INSALATE

INSALATE:
Authentic Italian
Salads for All Seasons

BY SUSAN SIMON
LOCATION PHOTOGRAPHY BY MANFREDI BELLATI
RECIPE PHOTOGRAPHY BY RICHARD ESKITE

CHRONICLE BOOKS
SAN FRANCISCO

For Musetta,
April 1988–May 2000,
il cane piu bella
al mondo,
she sure loved to
test recipes.

Library of Congress Cataloging-in-Publication Data:
Simon, Susan, 1945–
Insalate: Authentic Italian salads for all seasons / by Susan Simon;
photographs by Richard Eskite and Manfredi Bellati
p. cm.
Includes index
ISBN 0-8118-2872-7 (pbk.)
1. Salads. 2. Cookery, Italian. I. Title.
TX740.S469 20001
641.8"3"0945–dc21

Printed in China

Prop styling by Diane McGauley
Food styling by Sandra Cook
Designed by Deb Miner, designer
Typeset in Filosophia, Copperplate, and Avenir
Richard Eskite wishes to thank Leslie Busch, Melissa Castro, Juliann Harvey,
and Anne Tonai for their assistance on this book.

Distributed in Canada by Raincoast Books
9050 Shaughnessy Street
Vancouver, BC V6P 6E5

10 9 8 7 6 5 4 3 2 1

Chronicle Books LLC
85 Second Street
San Francisco, California 94105

www.chroniclebooks.com

Ci vuole quattro persone per fare un INSALATA
L'olio d'un prodigo
L'aceto d'un parsimonio
Il sale d'un saggio

E   rigirato
  mille volte   matto
       va   da un

Così si condisce l'insalata

You need four people to make a salad
One to add oil lavishly
One to add vinegar parsimoniously
One to add salt wisely
And a madman to toss it a thousand times
And that's how you dress a salad

INTRODUCTION

THE FIRST SALADS, AS WE KNOW THEM TODAY, were probably eaten in Italy when Greek colonists ate mixed fresh herbs. From the language of ancient Italy, Latin, comes the derivation of the word for *salad,* which is the word for salt: *sal.* Italian dictionaries give the first definition for salad as a dish made with greens dressed with *salt* and oil, and usually with vinegar or lemon as well. Salads made with other ingredients, and sweet salads, are variations on the original. The Italians have also given us a practical definition for salads by showing us how to make a salad with a single ingredient or a combination of ingredients bound together by a sauce.

In recent years, the trend in the United States has been to eat a salad at the end of a meal, European style—the idea being that it aids digestion. The Italians (as opposed to the French, who usually eat salads at the end of a meal, especially at home) have shown us how to start a meal, make a meal of, or end a meal with a salad. Italians may begin a meal with an antipasto or appetizer salad; they may eat *un piatto unico,* or a single-dish main-course salad; or they may have a simple *insalata* at the end of a meal.

The not-so-secret secret to a great salad, Italian style, is the ingredients. Fresh, in-season produce is the key to masterful Italian salads. I can't think of another country on earth whose population so reveres and appreciates vegetables and fruits, and so assiduously makes use of these foods in their *proper* season.

According to Greek and Roman mythology, it was the trials and tribulations of the goddess Persephone that gave birth to the calendar of seasons. Persephone (the beautiful daughter of Demeter, the goddess of agriculture and fertility, and Zeus, the king of the gods) was wandering in a meadow—thought to be in Sicily—when she was snatched by Hades and taken to the underworld to become his wife. The saddened and enraged Demeter took her revenge against the gods by refusing to let the crops grow. Zeus commanded the return of Persephone in order to return fertility to the earth. Unfortunately, while in the underworld Persephone had eaten pomegranate seeds, and with this act—the fruit symbolizes marriage—she became the wife of Hades. Now, it was up to Zeus to work out an arrangement between Demeter and Hades. In the agreed-upon compromise, winter became the season when Persephone stayed with Hades, while spring, summer, and fall were the seasons that she returned to her mother, and in those seasons the earth was fertile again.

It's precisely the diverse climates that provide the rich variety of produce in salads reflecting the seasons.

I began the research for this book with one big question: *"Cos'è l'insalata italiana* (What's an Italian salad)?" I asked all my Italian friends the same question, then my friend Antonia Jannone introduced me to the elegant, imperious Signor Carlo Ferrero. In the tiny, book-lined office located in the historic center of Milano that Sig. Ferrero shares with his companion, Signora Maria Paleari Henssler, my question began to be answered. Both Sig. Ferrero and

Sigra. Henssler are culinary historians, but it was very clear that Sig. Ferrero was in charge of our meeting. Impatient at first, he became generous with information, even copying whole pages of explanations and definitions from Italian culinary dictionaries and encyclopedias for me. The way he finally answered my "What is a salad?" question was pure drama, however—and in the end as exciting an answer as I could have hoped for. He opened a splendid old wooden cabinet, removed a fragile, leather-bound book, cradled it in his hands as if it were a newborn baby, and offered it to me to admire and examine. The book, *Archidipno, ovvero Dell'Insalata, e Dell'Uso di Esso (The First Course, or About Salad, About Its Use)* by Salvatore Massonio, was published in Venice in 1627. I could not have been more impressed and excited had Ferrero been Moses offering me the Ten Commandments. A single-subject book devoted to salads written in 1627! And a work of scholarship at that. The young Signor Massonio references the writings of more than one hundred authors, from Aristotle to Pliny the Elder, who wrote *Historia Naturalis* in the first century, to make his point about the importance of salad in the human diet. With chapters that ask "What Is Salad?" to fifty-seven (yes, Mr. Heinz, fifty-seven) chapters on individual ingredients from beets to truffles to sprouts to capers to tarragon, *e così via,* to the final chapter, "Useful Information About the Use of Salad."

My luck continued. It turned out that Sigs. Ferrero and Henssler had reprinted and annotated the original *Archidipno.* Their version is a beautiful book illustrated with antique botanical prints of salad plants. And now I own a copy.

Giacomo Castelvetro, another Italian chronicler of salads and their consequential benefits for human consumption, was a refugee from the Venetian Inquisition—he was a fiercely antipapal Protestant—living in England when he wrote a series of letters addressed to the citizens of his host country trying to persuade them to eat fresh food. In the letters, Castelvetro expresses his concern with the degrees of hygiene involved in salad preparation and told how to wash salad greens: with clean hands, in a bucket whose water is changed many times until not a speck of dirt remains in the bottom. He also gives salad-making directions: You may include mint, nasturtium, basil, citron, pimpernel flowers, tarragon, borage flowers and leaves, fennel sprouts, rosemary flowers, violets, and hearts of lettuce in order to ensure that it's pleasing, full of good flavor and fragrance. Dress it with salt and lots of oil. Finally, a word about how to eat a salad in the most gracious way: with a fork and knife. These hints from Castelvetro were written down in the early seventeenth century.

In the *Archidipno*, in the chapter about salad dressings, Massonio discusses the subtleties of the procedure. He writes that the way salad is dressed depends on its main ingredient. Bitter greens like chicory or endive need to be sweetened. Neutral greens like lettuce or borage leaves can take lots of flavor, and he lists pepper, orange juice, lemon juice, cooked must (back in fashion today as balsamic vinegar), garum, raisins, onion, garlic, and basil, in addition to olive oil and salt. Massonio believes that oil is added to salads to help evenly distribute the salt on the leaves. Of course.

The erudition of Massonio and Castelvetro leaves no doubt, at least in my mind, that a salad is one of the most ancient foods that we consume. The Greek colonist on Sicily who tossed together some of the wild herbs and greens that covered the island, ingeniously created the first salad and began a food tradition that evolved over time, from simple to ornate and elaborate. Salads composed for Medici princes, for example, were in the form of a tower made with wild herbs, greens, sprouts, candied oranges, breast of peahen, and pomegranate seeds, decorated with olives, capers, and nuts.

In the twentieth century, salads became simpler again. While the classic *insalata* does not stray far from the original salad made with fresh greens and wild herbs, the seventeenth-century salads of Massonio and Castelvetro include other vegetables, meat, fish, fruit, rice, and pasta, in combination with olives, anchovies, capers, nuts, and cheese, added to the salad greens. All the ingredients are then tossed with fine extra-virgin olive oil and aged balsamic vinegar, or olive oil and lemon juice—and salt.

Salt—ah, salt. The ingredient that gave salad its name is a *molto importante* salad ingredient. Hands down, I prefer sea salt. Briny, tingly tasting sea salt sparks all the foods that it touches. Surrounded by the Mediterranean Sea, the seaside towns of the Italian peninsula and her islands are home to many salt producers. Fittingly, a particularly prized sea salt comes from Sicily.

Extra-virgin olive oil is from olives that have been crushed, then pressed once through a mill. Extra-virgin olive oil must have an acidity level of less than 1 percent—and pass a taste test, which is completely subjective. Its flavor depends on the kind of olives used and where they were grown. Extra-virgin olive oil from Tuscany is distinct from the oil of Molise, which in turn is distinct from the oil of Sicily. In general, extra-virgin oil has a more robust flavor than oils that are further refined. I use extra-virgin olive oil when I want a strong oil flavor. When there are other ingredients in a salad that need to headline, I prefer to use regular olive oil, once called "pure" olive oil, which is actually a blend of extra-virgin and refined olive oils.

My favorite red wine vinegar is called *aspretto d'uvaggio di nobile:* a vinegar from the Tuscany of Da Vinci, made by fermenting "noble" grapes, distilling them, and adding *fresh* grape juice from the same fruit to the mixture, then aging the vinegar in wooden barrels for at least a year. Balsamic vinegar is made from must, or unfermented

grape juice; the best is aged in wooden barrels for decades, at least, if not for a century. There is lots of mass-produced, industrially aged balsamic vinegar on the market, too—and while its flavor doesn't come close to heady, rich, and smooth naturally aged balsamic vinegar, it does provide an alternative to sharper wine vinegars. Fresh lemon juice is also used all over Italy in combination with olive oil as a salad dressing—according to taste.

Massonio mentions garum as a condiment for salads. This stinky concoction, favored by the Romans as an all-purpose seasoning, was made with rotten fish intestines that were then macerated with salt until a kind of imperial Worcestershire sauce was achieved. I'm convinced that that Italian favorite, anchovy-and-oil salad dressing (see the very Roman salad, Puntarelle con Salsa d'Acciughe, page 82), is directly descended from garum.

Another, more modern dressing used to bind salad ingredients is mayonnaise. Mayonnaise is much loved by the Italians, who use it in mixed-vegetable, fish, and chicken salads, including their favorite, Insalata Russa (page 42).

Just as butter is used instead of oil for sautéing in the north of Italy, so is cream used instead of oil as a dressing for vegetable salads, especially in the Piemonte region, where it is often combined with mustard to make a dressing for Insalata di Fontina e Peperoni Gialli (page 96).

There was a time when Italy was truly exotic to the visitor. Americans were as fascinated and seduced by Italians and their lifestyle as the Italians were by the Americans. While the physical country, with its extraordinary and unique landscape and its villages, towns, cities, and buildings, is still a perpetual history lesson, the foods of everyday life, Italian style, are becoming as familiar to us as those made in the United States. It's not uncommon anymore to find a wide variety of imported Italian olive oils, vinegars, pastas, rices, and cheeses on supermarket shelves in this country. In the past few years, city greengrocers, farmers' markets, and countryside farm stands have proliferated here, offering unusual greens (some with Italian names!), several kinds of beets, many kinds of beans, herbs, and edible flowers, delighting the consumer and serving as a reminder of the bounty and variety of each season.

With all that's now available to us, why would anyone reach for a tomato in January, even if it's very red, in order to attempt to make an Insalata Caprese (page 53)? Why not grab some oranges and fennel and make an Insalata Palermitana (page 116) instead? Let the seasons be your guide to the best, most flavorful ingredients for your salads.

The pages of this book offer you a sampler of seasonal Italian salad recipes: Some are classics, some are adaptations of recipes from contemporary Italian cookbooks, and some are the favorite preparations of my Italian friends. The genius in all these deceptively simple recipes is that the main ingredients are fruits and vegetables that have matured and were harvested in their proper season. These unaffected and unintimidating salads are sure to please, whether they're eaten as a first course to stimulate the appetite, as a main course to sate the appetite, or at the end of a meal to aid with digestion.

BUON APPETITO!

1

Si sente la primavera: You feel springtime,

you smell springtime, you hear springtime, you taste springtime—

sentire is the Italian verb used to describe physical sensation.

There's no other Italian season that awakens the senses so fully.

The Italian spring starts in February in Sicily, when artichokes are

harvested in abundance, then rather quickly, on the wings of a warm

African breeze, it works its way up the peninsula, fanning the

fave of the Marches, the greens of the Roman countryside, and the

asparagus of the Veneto. Finally, it ends in an explosion of

pale pink apple blossoms in Alto Adige. Now, there are new foods

for the winter weary, and the earth is ready to be planted for the

summer harvest. *Primavera:* the first green. Springtime *all'italiana.*

INSALATA DI CARCIOFI

[Artichoke Salad]

4 large artichokes

1 whole lemon

¼ pound Parmesan cheese, shaved
with a mandoline or vegetable
peeler

3 tablespoons extra-virgin olive oil

2 tablespoons fresh lemon juice

2 tablespoons coarsely chopped
fresh flat-leaf parsley

Salt and freshly ground black
pepper to taste

SERVES 6 I landed in Italy for the first time in September 1965, when I went to study at L'Accademmia delle Belle Arti in Florence. In February 1966, a friend and I took a trip to Sicily, where we stayed in the beautiful resort town of Taormina. At every turn of that town's narrow, strictly pedestrian streets, there were unfamiliar, yet engaging things to see, smell, and taste. Of all the magnificent things that I encountered, nothing has stayed in my mind longer than the sight of children holding a whole artichoke in one hand, and tearing off the leaves to snack on with the other hand. Raw artichokes as a snack—what a concept! ⸎ From that time on, the artichoke harvest has been one I anxiously look forward to so I can make this classic raw-artichoke salad. ⸎ It's very often eaten with thinly sliced, raw beef fillet (carpaccio).

1. Prepare the artichokes: Cut the lemon in half. Squeeze both halves into a large bowl filled with water. Working with 1 artichoke at a time, cut the stem away from the base. Remove the outside leaves by bending them backward and pulling down; they'll snap at the "meaty" point of the leaf. Pull away the leaves until you see only the pale green ones, at about the halfway point of the artichoke. Use a very sharp knife to cut away the remaining leaf tops. Quarter the artichoke. Cut out the fuzzy choke. Using a very sharp knife or a mandoline, cut each quarter into very thin slices. Immediately add the slices to the lemon water to prevent them from turning brown. Continue this process until all the artichokes have been sliced.

2. Using a slotted spoon, transfer the artichoke slices from the lemon water to paper towels to drain for a few minutes. When they're dry, add them to a large bowl. Add the Parmesan shavings, olive oil, lemon juice, and parsley to the artichokes. Toss to thoroughly combine. Taste for salt and add with freshly ground pepper as needed. Serve immediately.

INSALATA DI FRUTTI DI MARE

[Seafood Salad]

1 cup steamed mussels (about
    4 pounds in their shells)
2 cups peeled and deveined
    medium-size boiled shrimp
    (about 1 pound)
1 cup cooked squid cut into ¼-inch
    rings (about 1 pound)
1 cup steamed and flaked firm,
    white-fleshed fish such as
    snapper (about 1 pound)
Grated zest and juice of 2 lemons
¾ cup finely chopped fresh flat-leaf
    parsley
¾ cup extra-virgin olive oil
½ teaspoon red pepper flakes
Salt and freshly ground black
    pepper to taste
Mixed greens for serving
Lemon wedges for garnish

SERVES 8 In late February (the start of Italian springtime) 1967, some friends and I drove from Milan to the Ligurian seacoast town of Sestri Levante for lunch. At Genoa, we left the Autostrada dei Fiori and turned onto a road that curves and snakes its way around—and sometimes through—the mountains that border the Mediterranean Sea, and headed toward Sestri Levante. As we passed through one town more charming than the next, the mimosa trees that lined the streets of the villages gave off a scent so powerful that it came into our car through closed windows and nearly intoxicated us. Thankfully, we arrived at our destination unscathed. Our many-coursed meal began with a seafood salad something like this one. This *insalata di frutti di mare* can be made with the ocean's offerings from any season, but, for me, it will always mean springtime.

1. In a large bowl, combine the mussels, shrimp, squid, and fish, lemon zest and juice, parsley, olive oil, and pepper flakes. Taste, then add salt and pepper as needed. Refrigerate for at least 2 hours and up to 4 hours before serving.

2. Serve on a bed of greens. Garnish each individual plate with a lemon wedge.

DUE DA CLEMY

[Two Salads from Clemy]

SERVES 6 *La signora* Clemy Vizzer is a vigilant guardian of her elegantly simple trattoria, Il Castelletto, tucked under a hill at Pedeguarda di Follina in the Veneto. The quintessential Italian mamma, Clemy, trailed by her fox terrier, Pozzo, patrols the rooms of the restaurant, checking that all her patrons have enough to eat. She gently commands her kitchen staff, and minutes later shiny white porcelain platters arrive at your table filled with surprises that are like her restaurant, elegant and simple. ᴧᴧ I'll never forget the first time I ate *spinaci con Gorgonzola.* It was early springtime, and the tender, young leaves, crisp and mineral, held their own under the warm, pungent, Gorgonzola bath. ᴧᴧ I was at Il Castelletto again one fall, anxious for a new Clemy creation, and she didn't disappoint when she brought out a big bowl of *spinaci con pancetta e uova.* ᴧᴧ To make these salads, choose firm baby spinach leaves in the cool of the early spring or fall.

SPINACI CON GORGONZOLA

[Spinach with Gorgonzola]

8 cups baby spinach leaves,
thoroughly washed and dried
½ pound mild Gorgonzola cheese
(dolcelatte)

1. Put the spinach in a large bowl.

2. In a double boiler over medium heat, melt the Gorgonzola until it's liquid. Pour over the spinach leaves and toss to thoroughly combine. Serve immediately.

SPINACI CON PANCETTA AFFUMICATA E UOVA

[Spinach with Bacon and Eggs]

3 hard-cooked eggs, halved
lengthwise
8 cups baby spinach leaves,
thoroughly washed and dried
½ pound smoked bacon, finely
diced
¼ cup extra-virgin olive oil
2 tablespoons balsamic vinegar
Salt and freshly ground black
pepper to taste

1. Separate the egg whites and yolks. Press the egg whites, then the yolks, through a sieve. Set aside.

2. Put the spinach in a large bowl.

3. In a medium skillet over medium heat, sauté the bacon until the pieces are brown and crisp. Pour off all but 1 tablespoon of the fat. Add the bacon and the tablespoon of fat to the spinach. Add the oil and vinegar. Toss to thoroughly combine. Taste for salt and add with freshly ground black pepper as needed. Toss again.

4. Cover the salad with the sieved eggs and serve immediately.

E UNA DA ANNA

[And One from Anna]

1 pink grapefruit, peeled and
    sectioned (see note)
3 tablespoons extra-virgin olive oil
1 teaspoon red wine vinegar
1 teaspoon salt
¼ teaspoon ground red hot pepper
8 cups baby spinach leaves,
    thoroughly washed and dried
2 tablespoons dried currants
2 tablespoons pine nuts

SERVES 6 A few years ago, in the last century (I like saying that), I was privileged to be a guest at Regaleali, the agricultural estate of the Tasca Lanza d'Almerita family in Sicily. Not only does Regaleali produce world-renowned wines, but it is also home to Marchesa Anna Tasca Lanza's World of Regaleali Cooking School. ⸻ It was early spring at the time of my visit and there was fresh citrus in abundance. The fruit appeared in almost all the food that we cooked and ate, from orange-scented potato purée to lemon-flavored *taralli* (hard biscuits) to smashed tangerines in green salads. ⸻ Anna loves to add citrus to salads. She talks about this salad in her memoir/cookbook, *The Heart of Sicily* (Clarkson Potter, 1993), where it is called Insalata di Spinaci alla Siciliana.

1. Put the grapefruit sections in a large bowl and lightly press them with a fork to extract some of the juice. Add the olive oil, vinegar, salt, and pepper and toss together to combine.

2. Add the spinach, currants, and pine nuts to the bowl. Toss together to thoroughly combine. Serve immediately.

PEELING AND SEGMENTING CITRUS FRUIT: Use a very sharp paring knife to peel away the skin, then the white pith from the fruit. Using the same sharp knife, carefully remove the segments one at a time by cutting between the fruit and the membrane. Remove the seeds from the segments.

ASPARAGI ALLA VENETA

[Asparagus Veneto Style]

2 pounds asparagus, trimmed and
    peeled
Four 8-minute hard-cooked eggs
Extra-virgin olive oil, red wine
    vinegar, salt, and freshly ground
    black pepper to taste for serving

SERVES 4 It's said that the asparagus from Bassano, in the Veneto, is just about the best-tasting stalk there is, though generally, it's the Veneti who expound the virtues of the labor-intensive-to-produce white asparagus. White asparagus grow in mounds of earth and need to be harvested with special tools that reach into the ground to pick them. Here's one thing that everyone agrees on: The Veneti know how to prepare asparagus. ⟂ Many towns celebrate the harvest with festivals, and restaurants devote entire menus to asparagus. This classic preparation is one that you'd be offered in every home from Bassano to Mestre and from Chioggia to Verona as a first-course salad. You can use white or green asparagus with equally good results.

1. In a large pot of boiling water, cook the asparagus for 2 minutes. Plunge into ice water to halt the cooking and drain on paper towels.

2. Divide the asparagus equally among 4 plates. Put a peeled hard-cooked egg on each plate. The diners should be instructed to chop or mash their egg and add olive oil, vinegar, salt, and pepper to taste, then eat the asparagus by dipping each stalk into and scooping up the egg mixture.

ASPARAGI ALLA CITRONETTE DI VERDURE

[Asparagus with Vegetable Citronette]

2 pounds asparagus, trimmed and
  peeled
¼ cup extra-virgin olive oil
2 tablespoons fresh lemon juice
½ teaspoon salt
¼ teaspoon freshly ground black
  pepper
1 carrot, peeled and minced
1 rib celery, peeled and minced
1 tablespoon minced shallot
2 teaspoons minced fresh chives
Arugula leaves for serving
  (optional)

SERVES 4 TO 6 Volumes have been written about the medicinal properties of asparagus. According to Pliny, author of *Historia Naturalis*, written in the first century A.D. and published in Venezia in 1469, if you eat asparagus, your belly will be soothed, and if you cook it in white wine, it will take care of chest, back, and intestinal pains. He warns us not to give the asparagus water to the dogs because it will kill them. I don't think I'll be testing that particular theory soon. ☰ The vegetable citronette (a dressing that uses citrus instead of vinegar) adds color, texture, and even more nutrition to the already super-healthful asparagus.

1. In a large pot of boiling water, cook the asparagus for 1 minute. Plunge into ice water to halt the cooking, then drain on paper towels.

2. In a large bowl, combine the olive oil, lemon juice, salt, and pepper and whisk together until emulsified. Fold in the carrot, celery, shallot, and chives.

3. Cut the asparagus into 1½-inch diagonal pieces. Add to the bowl. Toss to thoroughly coat the asparagus. Serve at room temperature, on a bed of arugula, if you like.

DUE CON FAVE

[Two with Fava Beans]

INSALATA CON FAVE E PECORINO

[Fava Beans with Sheep's Milk Cheese]

4 pounds fava beans, shelled
¼ cup extra-virgin olive oil
1 tablespoon fresh lemon juice
Salt and freshly ground black
    pepper to taste
½ pound fresh pecorino cheese
    (not the aged pecorino Romano
    used for grating)
1 loaf Mediterranean-style bread
    for serving

SERVES 4 Each spring, fava beans, resting in their plush-velvet pods, are as anxiously awaited as the first asparagus. In Emilia-Romagna and in Tuscany, the arrival of *fave* happily coincides with the arrival of fresh pecorino, a young sheep's-milk cheese. These two are a match made in heaven. This simple combination can open or close a meal.

1. In a large pot of boiling water, cook the fava beans for 2 minutes. Immediately plunge them into ice water to halt the cooking. Slip the skin off each bean. Put the beans in a large bowl and add the olive oil, lemon juice, and salt and pepper to taste. Toss together.

2. Divide the fava beans equally among 4 plates. Divide the cheese among 4 plates. Serve at room temperature with chunks of bread.

NOTE: If you can't find first-choice fresh favas, it's possible to find frozen ones in some Mediterranean and Middle Eastern grocery shops. Follow package directions for cooking and removing the skin.

FAVE ALLA VITALI

[Fava Beans Vitali Style]

4 pounds fava beans, shelled

½ pound smoked bacon, diced

2 tablespoons minced scallions
(white part only)

1 tablespoon chopped fresh mint

2 teaspoons red wine vinegar

2 tablespoons extra-virgin olive oil

Salt and freshly ground black
pepper to taste

SERVES 4 My friend Massimo Vitali—whom I call simply Vitali—is Marchegiano by heritage (from the Marches); however, I met him in the late 1960s in Milano, his adopted home at the time. He now lives in Lucca. Massimo is one of my gastronomic tour guides to Italy. With him and his retinue, I've floated down the Po River in a rubber raft to find just the right risotto, and have driven halfway down the Italian peninsula just to taste fried stuffed olives. And, oh, the food that comes out of his kitchen. *Buonissimo!* Fava beans are a particular favorite of the Marchegiani. Here's one way my favorite Marchegiano cooks them.

1. In a large pot of boiling water, cook the fava beans for 2 minutes. Immediately plunge them into ice water to halt the cooking. Slip the skin off each bean. Put the beans in a large bowl.

2. In a small skillet over medium heat, cook the bacon until brown and crisp. Using a slotted spoon, transfer to paper towels to drain. Add the bacon to the bowl.

3. Add the scallions, mint, vinegar, and olive oil to the bowl. Toss together to combine. Taste for salt and add with freshly ground pepper as needed. Serve at room temperature.

INSALATA SEMPLICE CON LATTUGA ROMANA E FINOCCHIO

[Simple Salad with Romaine Lettuce and Fennel]

¼ cup extra-virgin olive oil

2 teaspoons red wine vinegar

1 teaspoon dried oregano

1 teaspoon salt

¼ teaspoon freshly ground black
  pepper or ground red hot
  pepper

1½ cups thinly sliced fennel

6 tightly packed cups torn romaine
  lettuce

SERVES 4 TO 6 Cooking teacher Anna Tasca Lanza tells me that were you to visit any Sicilian household in late winter or early spring, this is the salad you would be served.

1. In a large bowl, combine the olive oil, vinegar, oregano, salt, and pepper. Whisk together until emulsified. Add the fennel and lettuce. Toss together. Serve immediately.

INSALATA ARLECCHINO

[Harlequin Salad]

1½ cups peeled and diced beets

⅓ cup extra-virgin olive oil

1 tablespoon fresh lemon juice

1 teaspoon salt

1 teaspoon freshly ground black
pepper

1½ cups thinly sliced fennel

1½ cups radishes, cut into matchsticks (see note)

1½ cups shredded carrots

1½ cups diced green bell pepper

SERVES 6 TO 8 This amusing salad, right out of the 1950s, comes from every Italian bride's first cookbook, *Il Cucchiaio d'Argento* (Editoriale Domus, *sesta edizione*, 1972). ⑉ The name *arlecchino* (harlequin) refers to the pattern that's created when the vegetables are arranged on a platter. This deceptively simple salad, with its colorful combination of vegetables, is full of complex flavor and texture. Serve it on a special occasion. Have fun with it.

1. In a medium saucepan fitted with a metal steamer, steam the beets until a tester easily passes through them. Remove and let cool.

2. In a small bowl, combine the olive oil, lemon juice, salt, and pepper. Whisk together until emulsified.

3. On a large platter, arrange the vegetables by group in triangular piles, with the point of the triangle directed toward the center of the platter. Be sure to alternate the colors in an attractive way. Drizzle all of the dressing over the vegetables. Serve immediately.

NOTE: To make radish matchsticks, cut radishes into very thin slices. Make piles of 6 or 7 slices, then julienne.

INSALATA RUSSA

[Russian Salad]

1¼ pounds yellow potatoes such as
    Yukon Gold or German
    Butterball, peeled and diced
1 cup peeled and diced beets
1 cup peeled and diced carrots
1 cup peas, the smaller the better
1 cup good-quality commercial
    mayonnaise
2 rounded tablespoons minced
    cornichons
1 rounded tablespoon minced
    capers
1 teaspoon grated lemon zest
1 tablespoon fresh lemon juice
Salt and freshly ground white
    pepper to taste

OPTIONAL GARNISHES:
Red and black caviar
Hard-cooked eggs
Fresh flat-leaf parsley sprigs
Boiled medium shrimp, shelled

SERVES 6 The Italian predilection for *maionese*-bound salads has made *insalata russa*, a Mediterraneanized version of a Russian potato salad (*salat olivet*) the king of the group. ⅏ Using the last of wintertime's root vegetables and the first springtime peas—or the first baby carrots, beets, and potatoes that start to appear sometime in midsummer, combined with frozen peas from the spring harvest—this salad will never disappoint. Whether you serve it as a first course, rolled up cornucopia style in a thin slice of baked ham, or sitting beside a piece of roast chicken, it's a potato salad as colorful as Red Square and as tasty as potato salad can be!

1. In a large saucepan fitted with a metal steamer, separately steam the potatoes, beets, carrots, and peas until a tester easily passes through them. Check the saucepan for water and add as needed. Put the vegetables in a large bowl and let cool.

2. Add the mayonnaise, cornichons, capers, lemon zest, and lemon juice to the vegetables. Carefully combine with a rubber spatula. The salad will take on a rosy glow, due to the beets. Taste for salt and add with pepper as needed.

3. Serve from the bowl, or turn the salad out onto a serving platter and form a mound. Decorate the mound with alternating circles or diamond shapes of red and black caviar, sliced hard-cooked eggs, and parsley sprigs. Or, simply surround the mound with a garland of boiled shrimp and parsley sprigs. The salad can be decorated up to 4 hours before serving. Refrigerate, then bring to room temperature to serve.

INSALATA REGINA
[The Queen's Salad]

½ pound potatoes, peeled and
diced

2 large carrots, peeled and diced

2 artichokes, trimmed and sliced
(see Step 1, page 25)

Tips from 1 pound asparagus

2 cups shredded romaine lettuce

1 cup cooked cannellini beans

2 tablespoons minced fresh
flat-leaf parsley

¾ cup good-quality commercial
mayonnaise

1 teaspoon salt

½ teaspoon freshly ground black
pepper

12 cornichons, cut into fans for
garnish

12 black olives, pitted for garnish

4 teaspoons capers for garnish

SERVES 8 The Duca di Salaparuta (1879–1946), who had many professions in his life, is remembered for his culinary endeavors. The Sicilian duke, a contemporary and friend of novelist Giuseppe di Lampedusa, was a vegetarian and naturalist, and the author of *La Cucina Vegetariana* (*The Vegetarian Kitchen*). He was also the director of the vineyard, founded by his grandfather, that produces the famous and prized Corvo di Salaparuta. This salad, the true queen to *insalata russa*, is from the duke's book and honors not only his chosen way of eating but also his aristocratic, Sicilian sense of style.

1. In a large saucepan fitted with a metal steamer, separately steam the potatoes, carrots, artichokes, and asparagus until a tester easily passes through them. Check the saucepan for water and add as needed.

2. In a large bowl, combine the potatoes, carrots, artichokes, asparagus, lettuce, beans, parsley, ½ cup of the mayonnaise, the salt, and pepper. Gently fold together with a rubber spatula.

3. Turn the salad out onto a serving platter and form a mound. Spread the remaining ¼ cup mayonnaise over the mound. Decorate the salad by making a border around the base with cornichon fans and olives. Sprinkle the capers over the top. Or, decorate as you like. Serve immediately.

INSALATA UMBRA

[Umbrian Salad]

1½ pounds potatoes, peeled and diced

1 cup peeled and diced beets

2 tablespoons extra-virgin olive oil

2 teaspoons red wine vinegar

1 teaspoon salt

¼ teaspoon freshly ground black pepper

1 cup good-quality commercial mayonnaise

6 ounces imported Italian canned tuna, drained and finely flaked

3 hard-cooked eggs, each cut into eighths lengthwise

1 tablespoon capers

¼ cup black olives, pitted

SERVES 6 This antipasto salad from Umbria completes the trio of *maionese* salads that the Italians love so much. This salad, like Insalata Russa (page 42), is one that you'll be likely to find at a *salumeria* (take-out food shop) or on a *tavola fredda* (a cold buffet table).

1. In a large saucepan fitted with a metal steamer, separately steam the potatoes and beets until a tester easily passes through them. Check the saucepan for water and add as needed.

2. In a large bowl, combine the potatoes, olive oil, vinegar, salt, and pepper. Set aside.

3. In a small bowl, combine the mayonnaise and tuna.

4. Turn the potatoes out onto a serving platter and form a mound. Cover the potatoes with the tuna mixture. Surround with the beets and egg wedges. Place the capers and olives over the top in a decorative way. Serve immediately.

RUCOLA CON PARMIGIANO E PINOLI

[Arugula with Parmesan and Pine Nuts]

3 tablespoons extra-virgin olive oil

2 teaspoons balsamic vinegar

6 tightly packed cups torn arugula
leaves

¼ pound Parmesan cheese, shaved
with mandoline or vegetable
peeler

1 teaspoon olive oil

2 tablespoons pine nuts

Salt and freshly ground black
pepper to taste

SERVES 4 TO 6 Called *rucola* in Italian, *rocket* in English, but *arugula* in markets and restaurants across the United States, this deep green leaf is practically synonymous with a whole new style of cooking and eating that invaded our country sometime in the early 1980s. According to my friend Massimo Vitali, an expert on food, among other things, this preparation for the overwintering arugula is a classic one. The sturdy, pungent, peppery leaf happily and deliciously accepts the nutty Parmesan and the smokey, crunchy pine nuts.

1. In a large bowl, combine the extra-virgin olive oil and vinegar. Add the arugula. Cover with the Parmesan.

2. In a small skillet over medium heat, heat the 1 teaspoon olive oil and sauté the pine nuts just until they begin to brown and smell like freshly popped corn. Remove from heat and add to the salad. Toss to combine. Taste and add salt and pepper as needed. Serve immediately.

INSALATA ITALO-SRI LANKA

[Italo-Sri Lankan Salad]

1 leek, trimmed to ¼ inch of the
green part

1 pineapple, peeled and quartered
lengthwise

1 napa cabbage (about 1 pound),
cored

½ pound carrots, peeled and cut
into 1½-inch matchsticks

¼ cup olive oil

1 teaspoon salt

SERVES 6 TO 8 It's hard to imagine a foreign cuisine infiltrating the determinedly chauvinistic Italian kitchen. The fairly recent influx of African and Asian immigrants to Italy, however, has begun—at least in private homes—to influence the way the natives eat. ⅏ This fresh, tangy salad is made for the Vitali family in Lucca by Roshan, their housekeeper from Sri Lanka. Employing salad-making methods and the all-important pineapple from his native island, he adds produce found at every Italian greengrocer. The cabbage he uses is a puckered-leaf variety called *verza*. I've substituted napa cabbage, with good results.

1. Cut the leek in half lengthwise and rinse it in a bowl of water, lifting the pieces up and down to make sure all the grit is removed. Rinse under running water. Drain on paper towels and pat dry. Cut the leek into 1½-inch matchsticks. Put them in a large bowl.

2. Cut the woody core from each quarter of the pineapple and discard. Cut each quarter into matchsticks. Add to the bowl.

3. Cut the cabbage into thirds crosswise. Finely slice. Add to the bowl.

4. Add the carrots, olive oil, and salt to the bowl. Toss to thoroughly combine. Serve at room temperature. The salad will keep in a tightly covered container in the refrigerator for up to 3 days.

INSALATA TRA STAGIONI

[Between-the-Seasons Salad]

1 seedless cucumber, peeled and
cut into ¼-inch dice

2 unpeeled Granny Smith apples,
quartered, cored, and cut into
¼-inch dice

2 ribs celery, peeled and cut into
¼-inch dice

2 teaspoons dried mint leaves

½ teaspoon salt

1½ cups (12 ounces) plain whole-
milk yogurt

SERVES 4 TO 6 My friend Miro sent me this recipe. He says it's just the kind of refreshing salad you can make with ingredients that are almost always in the market. Somewhere toward the end of March, when you've eaten oranges, cabbage, and radicchio up to your eyeballs and you're impatiently waiting for the first asparagus and baby spinach leaves, try this crunchy salad. It truly satisfies. Miro likes to eat it with a plain omelette for a light lunch.

1. In a large bowl, combine all the ingredients and fold together with a rubber spatula.

2. Refrigerate for at least 2 hours or as long as 24 hours before serving.

2

Tomatoes—sweetened by the intense heat of the Mediterranean

sun, and mouthwateringly fragrant, and succulent—signify

summertime in Italy. Tomatoes arrived in Italy in the

sixteenth century by a circuitous route that started in South America,

worked its way up to Mexico, then crossed the ocean to Europe with

the Spaniards. The journey from Spain to Italy was relatively easy.

The once-feared member of the deadly nightshade family

(the earliest ones were yellow, thus the name *pomodoro:* golden apple),

tomatoes may be one of the world's favorite foods.

The Italians have shown us many of the best ways to eat tomatoes,

including putting them in their world-class salads.

INSALATA CAPRESE

[Tomato and Mozzarella Salad]

Is it possible to put together a collection of Italian salad recipes and not include one for *insalata caprese*? I think that at least a *piccolo* explanation of this emblematic salad is in order. ᭫ This simple salad requires the best ingredients. It needs to be made in the season of melt-in-your-mouth vine-ripened tomatoes; fresh basil nurtured by sunshine; good-quality, fresh, moist, again, *moist*, mozzarella; genuine Italian extra-virgin olive oil; salt; and freshly ground black pepper. If you don't have these ingredients, you can't make a real *insalata caprese*. ᭫ This salad, which really was created on the island of Capri, off the coast of Naples, combines alternate slices of tomatoes and mozzarella, topped with torn basil leaves, a drizzle of olive oil, salt, and pepper. On Capri, it was, and is still, made with the locally available ingredients, including the *famossima* mozzarella di bufala, a specialty of the Campania region on the mainland. ᭫ Although the instructions for this salad are rather specific, if you follow them you *will* be rewarded.

INSALATA DI POMODORI CON SALSA DI POMODORI ALLA GABRIO BINI

[Gabrio Bini's Tomato Salad with Tomato Sauce]

TOMATO SAUCE:

1 clove garlic, minced

¼ cup extra-virgin olive oil

1½ pounds plum tomatoes, peeled and coarsely chopped

2 tablespoons coarsely chopped fresh basil

1 tablespoon red wine vinegar

Salt and freshly ground black pepper to taste

6 or 7 ripe tomatoes in assorted colors

Cherry tomatoes in assorted shapes, colors, and sizes for garnish

Whole fresh basil leaves for garnish

SERVES 6 If I were to credit one person with sending me off on my Italian food odyssey it would be Bruna Bini. The late Bruna, who opened her heart and her kitchen to me and made me part of her family, was my *mamma italiana*. I guess that makes her sons my brothers. The eldest son, Gabrio, inherited not only his mother's dramatic Etruscan good looks, but also her genius for making divine and imaginative food. No cookbook of mine would be complete without a Bini-inspired recipe. Gabrio answered my request for a salad recipe with this quirky and intensely tomatoey tomato salad.

1. Make the sauce: In a medium heavy-bottomed, nonreactive skillet over medium heat, sauté the garlic in the olive oil for about 30 seconds. Raise heat to high while adding the plum tomatoes.

2. Reduce heat and simmer the sauce until it is reduced by about one third, 20 to 30 minutes.

3. Remove from heat and add the basil, vinegar, salt, and pepper. Let cool and refrigerate for at least 2 hours, or until chilled.

4. To serve, cut the tomatoes into ¼-inch-thick slices. Arrange on a serving platter, alternating the colors. Generously spoon the chilled tomato sauce over the center of the slices. Garnish with cherry tomatoes and basil leaves.

INSALATA DEL BORGO DELLA VILLA BELLATI

[Summer Salad from the Villa Bellati]

Four 1½-inch-thick zucchini, cut
    into ¼-inch-thick diagonal slices

3 tablespoons extra-virgin olive oil

½ teaspoon salt

1 clove garlic, minced

4 ounces radish sprouts or other
    peppery sprouts

4 ripe red tomatoes, cut into ¼-
    inch-thick slices

¼ cup fresh basil leaves

SERVES 6 My friend Nally Bellati and I created this salad a few summers ago when I visited her and her husband, Manfredi, at their splendid country home in the *borgo* (hamlet) of Campea, not far from Venice. Nally loves to entertain, and she does so in grand style. Her beautifully decorated dining room is further adorned with delicious food presented on heirloom china or elaborate ceramic plates from the nearby factories in Bassano del Grappa. We came up with this salad because it used seasonal ingredients and it looked great on her new plates. ⺢ Sprouts, by the way, are historical Italian salad ingredients. Salvatore Massonio cites the use of mustard, turnip, mallow, horse-radish, and particularly hops sprouts in his *Archidipno, ovvero, Dell'Insalata*, written in 1627.

1. Prepare a fire in a charcoal grill, preheat a gas grill, or heat a cast-iron skillet over high heat for 1 minute.

2. Meanwhile, put the zucchini in a bowl. Add 2 tablespoons of the olive oil, the salt, and garlic and toss to thoroughly coat the zucchini.

3. Grill or sear the zucchini slices for about 30 seconds on each side, or until slightly golden and tender. Set aside.

4. Divide the sprouts equally among 6 plates. Place equal amounts of overlapping zucchini slices on top of the sprouts. Place equal amounts of overlapping tomato slices on top of the zucchini. Drizzle the remaining 1 tablespoon of olive oil over the tomatoes. Tear the basil leaves and strew them over the salads. Serve immediately.

NOTE: Nally likes to serve this salad with toasts covered with a local cheese called Crema del Piave, a soft cheese that's like Crescenza.

INSALATA ESTIVA ALLA SICILIANA

[Summer Salad, Sicilian Style]

4 ripe red tomatoes, cut into
   wedges and seeded

1 cucumber, peeled and cut into
   1-inch chunks

1 red onion, thinly sliced

1 tablespoon dried oregano

1 teaspoon salt

¼ teaspoon ground red pepper

3 tablespoons extra-virgin olive oil

SERVES 4 In summer, there's an abundance of incredibly flavored vegetables that beg for nothing more than *un filo*, a drizzle, of the best-quality olive oil and a sprinkle of crunchy sea salt to accompany them. This Sicilian-style summer salad is probably akin to something you already make with the season's first fragrant, warm-from-the-vine tomatoes. The addition of lots of dusky, aromatic oregano gives this salad its decidedly Sicilian imprimatur. And doesn't it remind you of those salads that are always served in little wooden bowls at neighborhood Italian restaurants?

1. In a large bowl, thoroughly combine all the ingredients.

2. Cover the bowl with plastic wrap and refrigerate for up to 1 hour. Toss again before serving.

INSALATA DI FARRO COME TABBOULEH ALLA MIRO

[Miro's Tabbouleh-like Farro Salad]

1¼ cups farro (spelt)

½ cup coarsely chopped fresh mint

1 cup coarsely chopped fresh
flat-leaf parsley

1 cup seeded and coarsely
chopped tomatoes

2 tablespoons finely chopped
onion

1 clove garlic, minced

3 tablespoons fresh lemon juice

3 tablespoons extra-virgin olive oil

1 teaspoon salt

SERVES 6 My friend Miro Silvera was born in Aleppo, Syria. He immigrated to Italy with his family when he was a young boy. Miro, a journalist and novelist, is at ease writing in French, English, and the language that he's made his own, Italian. Italianissimo Miro hasn't forgotten his roots. With this salad he's combined the favorite grain of Tuscany, farro, with the method for preparing the classic Middle Eastern salad, tabbouleh. The result is a perfectly refreshing summer salad. ⑭ Farro is called spelt in English. However, you will often find it for sale under the Italian name.

1. Cook the farro in a large pot of boiling water until al dente, 35 to 40 minutes. Drain and rinse in a colander under cold running water. Set aside to cool and drain.

2. Make sure the farro is dry—you may need to soak up excess dampness with paper towels. In a large bowl, combine the farro, mint, parsley, tomatoes, onion, garlic, lemon juice, olive oil, and salt. Toss to thoroughly combine. Let sit at room temperature for 30 minutes before serving. Taste for salt before serving and add as needed. Toss again, then serve.

PANZANELLA

[Bread Salad]

8 cups ½-inch cubes dense
    Mediterranean-style bread

4 cups ½-inch-diced fresh tomatoes

2 cups ½-inch-diced cucumbers

¼ cup coarsely chopped red onion

2 rounded tablespoons capers

½ cup extra-virgin olive oil

2 tablespoons red wine vinegar

2 tablespoons coarsely chopped
    fresh basil

2 teaspoons salt

1 teaspoon freshly ground black
    pepper, or to taste

OPTIONAL ADDITIONS:

Anchovies

Diced bell peppers

Fresh corn kernels

SERVES 8 Why is it that *la cucina dei poveri*—the food of the poor—always seems to be the savoriest? It must be because of its simple and uncomplicated ingredients, combined with the cook's sincere desire to both nourish and please. Panzanella is a dish typical of Tuscany and the province of Lazio (which has Rome as its capital city). Created to use up stale bread, which is soaked in cold water, then wrung dry, this salad needs only the addition of salt, olive oil, vinegar, and a chopped fresh herb such as parsley or basil to be authentic. It almost always includes chopped tomatoes and onions, however, as well as other tangy additions like anchovies or capers. My panzanella has cucumbers, too. ⑄ I also like to use toasted bread cubes instead of stale bread. The salad stays fresh longer, as the toast slowly absorbs the moisture from the vegetables and the oil. This way you can buy fresh bread just for the salad and not wait to have a quantity of stale bread.

1. Preheat an oven to 375°F. Evenly arrange the bread cubes on a baking sheet (you may need 2 sheets). Toast in the oven for 10 to 15 minutes, or until slightly golden, crunchy on the outside, and still soft on the inside. Let cool.

2. In a large bowl, combine the toasted bread, tomatoes, cucumbers, onion, capers, oil, vinegar, basil, salt, pepper, and any of the optional additions you like. Toss together to thoroughly combine. The salad can be made up to 1 hour before serving. Keep at room temperature.

INSALATA DI PASTA ALLA NALLY

[Nally's Pasta Salad]

2 pounds very ripe cherry tomatoes, stemmed and cut into
  quarters

½ cup fresh basil leaves, torn

1 clove garlic, minced

¼ cup extra-virgin olive oil

1 tablespoon balsamic vinegar

1 teaspoon sea salt (Nally uses fleur
  de sel)

1 pound dried pasta such as
  conchiglie, penne, fusilli

SERVES 4 TO 6 Italian pasta salads are simple dishes meant to showcase one main ingredient at a time, not everything but the kitchen sink like the pasta salads in the United States. Nally's recipe features incredibly sweet summer-harvested cherry tomatoes. True aficionados of this salad will set the covered bowl of the marinating tomatoes in the sun for an hour or so to allow the flavor to fully develop. ⸿ Although almost everyone in Italy makes this salad, for me, it will always be Nally's. She knows how much I love it, so it's invariably part of the first lunch she makes for me when I come to Italy for a visit.

1. In a large bowl, combine the cherry tomatoes, basil, garlic, olive oil, vinegar, and salt. Cover with plastic wrap and let marinate for at least 1 hour or up to 2 hours at room temperature and, preferably, in the sunshine.

2. In a large pot of salted boiling water, cook the pasta according to the package directions. Drain and rinse under cold running water. Set aside until dry.

3. Add the pasta to the tomato mixture and toss together to combine. Serve at room temperature.

INSALATA DI PASTA CON MELANZANE

[Pasta Salad with Eggplant]

1 large eggplant, cut into ½-inch
  dice (about 6 cups)

1 tablespoon kosher salt

½ cup olive oil

1 pound dried pasta such as
  conchiglie, fusilli, orecchiette

¼ cup minced fresh flat-leaf parsley

2 tablespoons pine nuts

Salt and freshly ground black
  pepper to taste

SERVES 4 TO 6 Here's another pasta salad that lets the main ingredient, eggplant, star. The other ingredients are the supporting cast. ⸎ Miro gave me this one, too. He added it as a postscript to a letter he sent to me. Eggplant was definitely on his mind. He began his note with "*Hai provato* (Have you tried) . . .? Delicious!" ⸎ Indeed.

1. In a large colander, combine the eggplant and kosher salt. Toss to coat the eggplant. Cover with paper towels and weight with a heavy object such as a cast-iron skillet. Let drain for 30 minutes. Rinse and pat dry with paper towels.

2. In a large skillet over medium-high heat, heat ¼ cup of the olive oil and fry the eggplant in small batches until the pieces are brown and crisp, about 1½ minutes (cooking too much eggplant at once will result in boiled, not fried pieces). Using a slotted spoon, transfer to paper towels to drain. Continue until all the eggplant is cooked. Let cool.

3. In a large pot of salted boiling water, cook the pasta according to the package directions. Drain and rinse under cold running water. Set aside until dry.

4. In a large bowl, combine the pasta, eggplant, and parsley.

5. In a small skillet over medium heat, heat the remaining ¼ cup olive oil and sauté the pine nuts until they begin to brown and smell like freshly popped corn. Remove from heat and immediately add to the other ingredients. Toss together. Taste for salt and add with pepper as needed. Toss again and serve at room temperature.

INSALATA DI RISO

[Rice Salad]

1½ cups Carnaroli or a long-grain rice, cooked, drained, and cooled

1 cup diced Emmentaler cheese

6 ounces imported Italian canned tuna packed in oil, drained and flaked

4 hard-cooked eggs, diced

1½ cups chopped ripe tomatoes

2 tablespoons capers

2 tablespoons minced cornichons

2 tablespoons chopped fresh basil

¼ cup extra-virgin olive oil

1 teaspoon salt

Freshly ground black pepper to taste

SERVES 6 TO 8 Italy is indisputably the rice-growing capital of Europe—the grain was brought to Sicily in the eleventh century when the Saracens invaded. The cultivation of rice was eventually concentrated in the northern part of the country, with its more hospitable terrain and better access to fresh water. In 1787, when Thomas Jefferson was the American ambassador to France, he took an arduous, kidney-jostling coach journey to Italy for the sole purpose of procuring rice to bring back to the United States to cultivate on his Virginia plantation. With this act he risked the punishment of death, the United States penalty at that time for the importation of foreign seeds. It is entirely possible that during his journey Ambassador Jefferson may have dined on a version of this rice salad, as Italians eat rice salads year-round. The rice of choice for a salad is the superfino, even-cooking carnaroli. If Carnaroli is not available, a long-grain rice can be used. A rice salad can be a tasty first course, or a warm-weather *piatto unico*, one-dish meal.

1. Put the rice in a large bowl. Add all the remaining ingredients and gently fold together with a rubber spatula. Serve immediately, or cover with plastic wrap and refrigerate until 30 minutes before serving. Serve at room temperature.

INSALATA DI RISO AL BISANZIO

[Byzantine Rice Salad]

3 very ripe large tomatoes, coarsely
  chopped
1 clove garlic, mashed through a
  press
1 tablespoon capers
2 tablespoons chopped fresh basil
¼ cup extra-virgin olive oil
1 tablespoon red wine vinegar
1 teaspoon salt
½ teaspoon freshly ground pepper
1½ cups Carnaroli or a long-
  grained rice, cooked, drained,
  and cooled
1 cup shaved Parmesan cheese

SERVES 6 When used in conjunction with food, *bisanzio* means "dressed with tomatoes."

1. In a medium bowl, combine the tomatoes, garlic, capers, basil, olive oil, vinegar, salt, and pepper. Stir to mix. Let sit, uncovered, for at least 30 minutes or up to 1 hour.

2. Add the rice to a large bowl. Add the tomato mixture and stir to thoroughly combine. Serve immediately, garnished with the Parmesan cheese.

CONDIJUN

6 to 8 hardtack biscuits (*gallette da marinaio*, or *taralli*) (see note)

2 cloves garlic, halved

4 tablespoons extra-virgin olive oil

2 teaspoons red wine vinegar

Pinch of salt

¼ cup water

2 large, very ripe red tomatoes, cut into ¼-inch slices

1 cucumber, peeled and thinly sliced

1 yellow bell pepper, seeded, de-ribbed, and cut into ¼-inch-wide strips

1 red onion, thinly sliced

4 cups Boston lettuce leaves, torn

2 hard-cooked eggs, sliced into rounds

6 anchovy fillets

3 tablespoons Taggia or niçoise olives

¼ cup fresh basil leaves

Sea salt for serving

SERVES 6 *Condijun* is Ligurian dialect for *condiglione*, a huge mixed salad. It's one of the few authentic main-course salads from the Italian kitchen. Like so many traditional dishes, the ingredients vary according to the maker. I've read dozens of condijun recipes, and while some require *gallette da marinaio* (hardtack); *bottarga*, the salted, pressed roe of mullet or tuna; and the small Taggia olives of the region, some use hard-cooked eggs and anchovies. Some add it all. All versions of condijun are eaten in the same way, however. The salad is served in a large bowl placed in the center of the table. Diners eat directly from the bowl, creating a convivial atmosphere.

1. Rub the biscuits with the garlic. Put them in a bowl and add 3 tablespoons of the olive oil, 1 teaspoon of the vinegar, the salt, and water. Toss to thoroughly coat the biscuits. Let sit for 10 minutes.

2. Break each biscuit into 4 pieces and put in a large salad bowl. Add the tomatoes, cucumber, pepper, onion, lettuce, remaining 1 tablespoon olive oil, and remaining 1 teaspoon vinegar. Toss to combine.

3. Decorate the top of the salad with the eggs, anchovies, olives, and basil. Let sit for 10 to 15 minutes before serving. Serve with tiny dishes of sea salt to add as needed.

NOTE: *Gallette da marinaio*, or *taralli*, are often available at Italian bakeries.

INSALATA DI MISTICANZA

[Salad of Wild Greens and Herbs]

I have a clear summertime memory from my childhood in Stamford, Connecticut, of bent-over middle-aged men and women searching alongside roads and in fields for wild greens. I learned that the plants were dandelion greens. Those men and women, mostly Italian immigrants, were the grandparents and parents of my contemporaries. The hunt for wild greens is an activity as old as the Roman Empire, when citizens roamed the countryside looking for dandelion leaves as well as wild chicory, asphodel, chervil, calendula, mallow, mustard, pimpernel, purslane, borage, and wild fennel to bring home to make into salads. The Romans were so fond of their salads that this one, which is still popular all over central and southern Italy, is sometimes called *insalata d'erbe romane*. ⚜ While you may not be able to find pimpernel and asphodel in your local market, or for that matter in the field next door, you'll probably be able to find dandelion, borage, purslane, and calendula petals in some farmers' markets and natural foods stores. ⚜ A salubrious salad of mixed wild greens and herbs can be dressed simply with olive oil, fresh lemon juice or vinegar, salt, and pepper—or slightly more elaborately with anchovies and garlic cooked in olive oil in a small skillet over low heat until the anchovies dissolve. Add vinegar to the mixture and pour over the greens.

INSALATA PANTESCA

[Tomato and Potato Salad from Pantelleria]

1½ pounds new potatoes, cut into
  ½-inch pieces
1 pound tomatoes, halved, seeded,
  and coarsely chopped
¼ cup finely diced red onion
¼ pound smoked bluefish, or other
  smoked fish, finely flaked
2 tablespoons capers
½ cup firmly packed coarsely
  chopped fresh flat-leaf parsley
½ cup extra-virgin olive oil
¼ pound dense Mediterranean
  bread, soaked in water for 15
  minutes and squeezed dry
Salt to taste

SERVES 6 When Gabrio Bini gave me a couple of jars of salt-preserved capers from his property on Pantelleria—a sun-drenched volcanic island between Sicily and Tunisia—he gave me explicit instructions for making this salad as well. The traditional version calls for a tiny fish found only near Pantelleria. I included this recipe in my book *The Nantucket Table* (Chronicle Books, 1998), substituting smoked bluefish for the local fish.

1. Cook the potatoes in abundant boiling water until a tester easily passes through them. Drain and plunge into ice water to halt the cooking. Dry on paper towels.

2. In a large bowl, combine the potatoes, tomatoes, onion, fish, capers, parsley, and olive oil. Crumble the dried bread and add to the mixture. Toss together. Taste for salt (the capers and smoked fish are salty) and add as needed. Toss again, and serve.

PATATE E FAGIOLINI AL PESTO

[Potatoes and Green Beans with Pesto]

PESTO:

1 cup fresh basil leaves

1 tablespoon pine nuts

1 clove garlic

1 tablespoon grated Parmesan
   cheese

1 teaspoon salt

½ cup extra-virgin olive oil

1½ pounds new potatoes, cut into
   1-inch pieces

1 pound haricots verts or full-size
   green beans, trimmed and cut
   into thirds crosswise

SERVES 6 From the Liguria region on Italy's west coast comes this recipe that combines pesto and one of the all-time favorite Italian salads, potatoes and green beans. I like to use the skinny haricots verts when making this salad. Their shape and texture is a little closer to the Italian *fagiolini* than our fatter green beans.

1. Make the pesto: Combine the basil, pine nuts, garlic, Parmesan, and salt in a blender or food processor. With the machine running, drizzle in the olive oil and process for a few seconds until the basil is coarsely chopped. Pour into a bowl and set aside. (The pesto can be made ahead and refrigerated in a tightly covered container for up to 4 days; bring to room temperature for use.)

2. Cook the potatoes in abundant boiling water until a tester easily passes through them. Drain and plunge into ice water to halt the cooking. Drain and pat dry with paper towels.

3. Blanch the beans in boiling water for 30 seconds. Plunge into ice water to halt the cooking. Drain and pat dry with paper towels.

4. In a large bowl, combine the potatoes, beans, and pesto. Toss together to thoroughly combine. Serve at room temperature.

CAPONATA ALLA SICILIANA

[Sicilian Caponata]

2 unpeeled medium eggplants,
   cut into ¾-inch cubes (10 cups)

1 tablespoon kosher salt

2 onions, coarsely chopped

½ cup extra-virgin olive oil

1½ pounds plum tomatoes, peeled
   and coarsely chopped

2 ribs celery, peeled and cut into
   ½-inch half-moons

3 tablespoons tomato paste, mixed
   with ½ cup boiling water

Olive oil for frying

Leaves from 1 bunch celery,
   coarsely chopped

½ cup red wine vinegar

2 tablespoons sugar

1 cup coarsely chopped green
   olives

⅓ cup capers

2 tablespoons pine nuts

Salt and freshly ground black
   pepper to taste

Coarsely chopped fresh flat-leaf
   parsley for garnish

SERVES 8 Caponata can be many different salads in Italy—it all depends on the region. I think all of them are descendants of the Genovese caponata, which is made with oil-and-vinegar-soaked hardtack dressed with capers and anchovies: a meal of preserved foods, perfect for the sea-faring Genovese population. The Sardinians, who were major traders with the Genovese, added preserved tuna and tomatoes. The Insalata di Rinforzo (page 109) is very often called caponata—its main ingredient is cauliflower—but it's dressed in the same way as the Genovese salad. ⺡ Here's the Sicilian caponata, made with the stars of late-summer, eggplant and tomatoes.

1. In a large colander, combine the eggplant and kosher salt. Toss to coat the eggplant. Cover with paper towels and weight with a heavy object such as a cast-iron skillet. Let drain.

2. Meanwhile, make the sauce: In a large nonreactive saucepan over medium heat, sauté the onions in the ½ cup olive oil until translucent. Add tomatoes, sliced celery, and tomato paste mixture. Reduce heat and simmer.

3. Rinse and dry the drained eggplant. Add 3 tablespoons olive oil to a large skillet over medium heat and fry the eggplant in batches until golden and crisp, 2 or 3 minutes. Add more olive oil as needed. Using a slotted spoon, transfer to paper towels to drain.

4. Add the eggplant, celery leaves, vinegar, sugar, olives, capers, pine nuts, salt, and pepper to the sauce. Simmer for 15 to 20 minutes, stirring occasionally. Transfer to a glass or ceramic bowl to cool. Serve at room temperature, garnished with chopped parsley, or store in a tightly covered container in the refrigerator for up to 2 months.

INSALATA DI FRUTTI DI BOSCO CON SALSA DI MIRTILLI

[Mixed Berry Salad with Blueberry Sauce]

8 ounces fresh blueberries, rinsed
and picked over

1 tablespoon honey

1 tablespoon fresh lemon juice

1½ pounds assorted fresh berries
(raspberries, blueberries,
blackberries, strawberries, etc.)

SERVES 6 Made with the renowned apple-blossom honey of the Alto Adige region of Italy, the blueberry sauce for this salad adds just enough sweetness to balance the tartness of the berries. ⅏ I'm not ashamed to say that I love to serve this berry salad with ice cream, heavy cream, mascarpone, frozen yogurt . . . *e così via*.

1. In a small saucepan over medium heat, combine the 8 ounces blueberries, the honey, and lemon juice. Cook over medium heat, stirring occasionally, until the berries release their juice, about 3 minutes. Remove from heat and let cool.

2. In a large bowl, combine the mixed berries and the blueberry sauce. Toss together. Serve at room temperature, or store in a tightly covered container in the refrigerator for up to 3 days.

3

If summertime in Italy is defined by the heat of the sun, then it's the

cool, damp earth that gives fall its definition. Piles of fallen leaves

around the base of a chestnut tree or in a deserted vineyard hide a

treasure of mushrooms and truffles waiting to be collected.

Mounds of freshly dug potatoes, celery root, and Jerusalem artichokes,

dirt still clinging to them, decorate the entrances to the greengrocers.

And fields patterned by swaths of just-harvested rice plants

prompt thoughts of the great salads to come.

VERDURE IN AGRODOLCE

[Sweet and Sour Vegetables]

SWEET AND SOUR SAUCE:

1 cup white wine vinegar

½ cup sugar

2 tablespoons kosher salt

1 whole dried cayenne pepper

3 pounds fresh plum tomatoes, peeled, or canned peeled plum tomatoes

1 eggplant, peeled and cut into ½-inch dice (2 cups)

2 carrots, peeled and cut into ¼-inch-thick rounds

2 ribs celery, peeled and cut into 1-by-½-inch sticks

1 large bulb fennel, trimmed and cut lengthwise, then into ½-inch pieces

2 artichokes, trimmed and thinly sliced (see Step 1, page 25)

2 bell peppers (1 green, 1 yellow), seeded, deribbed, and cut into 1-inch triangles

2 cups cauliflower florets (1 head)

¼ pound green beans, trimmed and cut into 1½-inch pieces

2 zucchini, cut in half lengthwise, then into ½-inch pieces

15 pearl onions, peeled

Salt to taste

MAKES 3½ QUARTS I had to think for a while about which season this recipe should be part of; I decided on fall because I ate this salad for the first time in November, in Italy, when Loredana Lazzarini gave it to me to taste. The vegetables in this sweet-and-sour preparation are all available in the United States at about the same time of year. ⸾⸾⸾ This preparation is good for other seasons, too. In fact, Loredana makes it in the summertime, substituting some vegetables for others, and adds flaked, canned tuna and black olives to make what she calls *"un piatto unico estivo,"* a one-dish summertime meal.

1. In a large stockpot, combine the vinegar, sugar, kosher salt, and cayenne pepper. Bring to a boil over medium heat. Add the tomatoes and cook for 5 minutes, stirring occasionally.

2. Stir in the eggplant, carrots, celery, fennel, and artichokes. Cook for 10 minutes, stirring occasionally.

3. Stir in the bell peppers, cauliflower, and green beans. Cook for 10 minutes, stirring occasionally.

4. Stir in the zucchini and onions. Cook for 15 minutes, stirring occasionally. Taste for salt and add as needed. Transfer the mixture to a ceramic or glass bowl and let cool. Serve immediately, or refrigerate in tightly covered containers for up to 2 weeks.

INSALATA DI MELANZANE

[Eggplant Salad]

8 cups water

¼ cup red wine vinegar

2 eggplants, peeled and cut into
½-inch dice (about 10 cups)

¼ cup extra-virgin olive oil

1 clove garlic, minced

1 teaspoon salt

¼ teaspoon ground red hot pepper

2 tablespoons coarsely chopped
fresh mint

SERVES 6 "Eggplant and fennel forty years ago were just beginning to be seen in the market in Florence; until then they were considered the vile food of the Jews." So wrote Pellegrino Artusi in 1891 in his seminal book, *Culinary Science and the Art of Eating Well.* Artusi's classic work doesn't have a single eggplant preparation among the over 750 recipes. Can you imagine Italian cuisine without eggplant? ⫙ Now, eggplant is ubiquitous—especially in the southern part of the country, where it's used in pasta, stews, and salads. My Roman friend, *cuoca per eccelenza* Ester Bini, makes this salad in the fall as a way of preserving end-of-the-summer eggplant. She kindly shared her recipe with me.

1. In a large pot over medium heat, combine the water and vinegar. Bring to a boil. Add the eggplant in small batches, cooking each batch for 4 minutes and occasionally pressing the pieces down into the liquid with a wooden spoon to ensure that all the pieces cook. Using a slotted spoon, transfer to paper towels to drain.

2. In a small bowl, combine the olive oil, garlic, salt, and pepper and whisk together.

3. Using your hands, gently squeeze the excess liquid from the eggplant. Put the eggplant in a large bowl. Add the olive oil mixture and mint. Toss to thoroughly combine. Serve at room temperature. Store in the refrigerator for up to 1 month by floating a thin layer of olive oil over the top.

PUNTARELLE CON SALSA D'ACCIUGHE

[Puntarelle with Anchovy Sauce]

1½ pounds chicory

2 cloves garlic

2 or 3 anchovy fillets

1 tablespoon fresh lemon juice

1 teaspoon red wine vinegar

3 tablespoons extra-virgin olive oil

Salt and freshly ground black
    pepper to taste

SERVES 4 TO 6 Starting in the autumn and continuing throughout the winter, puntarelle, whose origins are Roman, is one of Italy's favorite salads. It's made with the ribs of wild chicory, or *catalogna*, an ingredient not easily found in the United States. I've made this salad using the ribs of regular old supermarket chicory, and the results are delicious. The important thing is that the salad be crunchy, salty, and garlicky.

1. Remove all the leaves from the ribs of the chicory. Reserve for another use, such as soup. Rinse the ribs and cut them into 3- to 4-inch pieces. Split the tips of each rib piece by about ½ inch. Soak the pieces in a large bowl of ice water for at least 30 minutes or up to 2 hours. The pieces will lose some of their bitterness and curl up.

2. Add the garlic and anchovies to a mortar and use a pestle to mash the ingredients into a paste. Gradually mix in the lemon juice, vinegar, and olive oil to make a smooth, creamy dressing.

3. Remove the chicory ribs from the ice bath and pat dry with paper towels. Transfer to a large bowl. Pour on the dressing and toss to thoroughly combine. Taste for salt and add with freshly ground black pepper as needed. Serve immediately.

DUE CON SEDANO DI VERONA

[Two with Celery Root]

INSALATA CAPRICCIOSA

[Capricious Salad]

1¼ pounds celery root, peeled and
shredded (about 3 cups)

2 tablespoons fresh lemon juice

½ pound Genoa salami, cut into
2-by-¼-inch sticks

½ pound boiled ham, cut into
2-by-¼-inch sticks

½ pound Gruyère or Emmentaler
cheese, cut into 2-by-¼-inch
sticks

½ cup diced marinated mushrooms

½ cup good-quality commercial
mayonnaise

Freshly ground white pepper to
taste

Coarsely chopped fresh flat-leaf
parsley for garnish

SERVES 8 The Piemontese kitchen is particularly proud of its end-less antipasto offerings. It's not unusual to begin a dinner in Torino with ten or twelve different *antipasti*. This always-included *insalata capricciosa* is usually made with pickled tongue. For this recipe, I've substituted the more widely available Genoa salami.

1. In a large bowl, combine the celery root and lemon juice and toss to-gether well (besides adding flavor, the lemon juice will keep the celery root from turning brown).

2. Add the salami, ham, cheese, mushrooms, mayonnaise, and pepper. Fold together with a rubber spatula to combine. Serve immediately, gar-nished with parsley, if you like. Or, refrigerate in a tightly covered container for up to 4 days. Toss again with a rubber spatula before serving.

SEDANO DI VERONA ALLA FRANCESE

[French-Style Celery Root Salad]

2 pounds celery root, peeled and
   shredded
1 tablespoon fresh lemon juice
¾ cup good-quality commercial
   mayonnaise
3 tablespoons Dijon mustard
3 tablespoons minced fresh flat-
   leaf parsley
½ teaspoon salt
½ teaspoon freshly ground white
   pepper
Belgian endive leaves for garnish
   (optional)

SERVES 8 Sedano di Verona, as its name implies, is a crop grown in Northern Italy. This classic French-style preparation is widely used in the Veneto region, where Verona is located. ⫿⫿⫿ I like to serve this salad with endive leaves; the presentation is attractive, and the leaves can be used to scoop up the salad.

1. In a large bowl, combine the celery root and lemon juice and toss well.

2. Add the mayonnaise, mustard, parsley, salt, and pepper. Fold together with a rubber spatula to combine. Serve immediately, surrounded by endive leaves, if you like. Or, refrigerate in a tightly covered container for up to 4 days.

INSALATA DI ZUCCA

[Squash Salad]

3 whole cloves

1½ to 1¾ pounds butternut or
   Hubbard squash, peeled,
   seeded, and cut into 1-inch
   chunks

1 red onion, cut into eighths

4 teaspoons capers

2 tablespoons olive oil

2 tablespoons pine nuts

Grated zest and juice of 1 orange

1 tablespoon Dijon mustard

1 teaspoon salt

½ teaspoon freshly ground black
   pepper

SERVES 6 I found the chapter on squash in the *Archidipno, ovvero Dell'Insalata* fascinating. Salvatore Massonio writes that Pliny had a lot to say about squash, and in the same breath he tells us that squash is easy to digest, that it quenches thirst, and that it goes well with the following condiments: oregano, mustard, and saffron. He also describes a way of dressing squash with oil, pepper, and orange juice. ⅏ This recipe is a combination of one that I found in an Italian cookbook printed 350 years after the *Archidipno*, and Massonio's advice.

1. Place the cloves in a large saucepan, add water, and fit it with a metal steamer. Over medium heat, steam the squash and onion for about 15 minutes, or until a tester easily passes through them. Remove from the steamer and let cool.

2. Put the squash in a large bowl. Coarsely chop the onion and add to the bowl. Add the capers.

3. In a small skillet over medium heat, heat 1 tablespoon of the olive oil and sauté the pine nuts until they begin to brown and smell like freshly popped corn. Remove from heat and add to the squash mixture.

4. In a small bowl, combine the remaining 1 tablespoon olive oil, the orange zest and juice, mustard, salt, and pepper and whisk together until emulsified. Add to the large bowl and toss with the other ingredients to thoroughly combine. Let sit at room temperature for at least 30 minutes or up to 1 hour before serving. To store, refrigerate in a tightly covered container for up to 2 days.

INSALATA DI SEDANO

[Celery Salad]

Ribs from 1 bunch celery, peeled
   and thinly sliced into chevrons
   (about 4 cups)
⅓ cup walnuts, coarsely chopped
¼ pound Emmentaler cheese, cut
   into 1-inch-long matchsticks
1 tablespoon fresh lemon juice
2 tablespoons olive oil
2 tablespoons heavy cream
½ teaspoon salt
Freshly ground white pepper to
   taste

SERVES 6 I had almost forgotten how good a celery salad can be until Marijke Cavalchini reminded me. It was then that I flashed back to the sunny autumn afternoon in Mantova, many years ago, when I tasted my first celery salad, Italian style. It was served as part of an antipasto plate at a trattoria just across the piazza from the Mantegna-filled Palazzo Ducale. If my memory is correct, there was a mushroom salad and a few paper-thin slices of salty-sweet *prosciutto crudo* on the plate as well. ⅏ This celery salad does indeed work well in combination with other salads.

1. In a large bowl, combine the celery, walnuts, and cheese.

2. In a small bowl, combine the lemon juice, olive oil, cream, salt, and pepper. Whisk together until emulsified. Add to the celery and toss together to thoroughly combine. Serve as part of an antipasto selection. Or, refrigerate in a tightly covered container for up to 3 days. Bring to room temperature before serving.

INSALATA DI SCAROLA

[Escarole Salad]

6 tightly packed cups torn escarole leaves

¼ pound Parmesan cheese, finely diced

2 tablespoons capers

1 teaspoon olive oil

3 tablespoons coarsely chopped hazelnuts

2 tablespoons extra-virgin olive oil

2 tablespoons heavy cream

1 tablespoon fresh lemon juice

Salt and freshly ground pepper to taste

SERVES 6 Escarole, a member of the chicory group of cool-weather salad greens, has a broad, more lettucelike leaf than the other members of its family, and a slightly less bitter taste as well. Even more important to the cook, escarole is a relatively easy-to-find ingredient. There's lots of flavor and texture going on in this salad. I recommend serving it with a simple piece of grilled fish, or a chicken breast—call it dinner. *Basta.*

1. In a large bowl, combine the escarole, Parmesan, and capers.

2. Add the 1 teaspoon olive oil to a small skillet over medium heat, then add the hazelnuts. Sauté, moving the nuts around with a wooden spoon until they become bronze and smell like freshly popped corn, about 90 seconds. Add them to the escarole.

3. In a small bowl, combine the extra-virgin olive oil, heavy cream, and lemon juice and whisk together until emulsified. Add to the escarole mixture and toss together to thoroughly combine. Taste for salt—the Parmesan and capers are salty—and add with freshly ground white pepper as needed. Toss again and serve immediately.

INSALATA DI FUNGHI MISTI

[Mixed Mushroom Salad]

½ cup thinly sliced shallots

¼ cup olive oil

2 pounds assorted mushrooms
such as cremini, portobello, or
shiitake, dusted off and thinly
sliced

1 tablespoon fresh lemon juice

½ cup coarsely chopped fresh
flat-leaf parsley

1 teaspoon salt

Freshly ground pepper to taste

6 cups mixed salad greens

3 tablespoons olive oil

1 teaspoon red wine vinegar

Croutons (recipe follows)

SERVES 6 Lucia Piccini, the very talented young chef at the Hotel Abbazia's restaurant, Alla Corte, generously shared her recipe for mushroom salad with me. I ate it on the first night of a week-long stay in the Veneto in November a few years ago. I was looking forward to infinite amounts of the renowned Italian mushrooms and truffles that are on everyone's menu in the fall. Luckily for me, Lucia's salad was the first one I ate, because the next day I ordered a mushroom salad in a little restaurant near Padova and became ill from it. When I told Lucia what happened, she said that even though raw mushroom salads are everywhere—and really tasty—she always gives the funghi a quick sauté before serving them. "Mushrooms are quite porous, and you never know who's touched them," she said. ⁓ I've made this salad with cultivated mushrooms. If wild mushrooms are available at your local market, however, by all means use them.

1. In a large skillet over medium heat, sauté the shallots in the ¼ cup olive oil until translucent, about 90 seconds. Increase heat to high and add the mushrooms. Sauté for about 30 seconds, stirring with a wooden spoon. Remove from heat and put in a large bowl.

2. Add the lemon juice, parsley, salt, and pepper. Toss to thoroughly combine. Dress the greens with the oil and vinegar. Serve surrounded with the croutons.

CROUTONS: Preheat an oven to 350°F. Cut a baguette into ¼-inch-thick slices. Brush the entire surface of a baking sheet with a bit of corn oil. Place the bread slices on the sheet. Brush each slice with a bit of corn oil. Bake until the slices are golden, about 10 minutes.

INSALATA DI TOPINAMBUR
[Jerusalem Artichoke Salad]

½ cup heavy cream

Juice of 2 lemons, plus 1 tablespoon fresh lemon juice

1¼ pounds Jerusalem artichokes
(sunchokes)

2 tablespoons olive oil

6 anchovy fillets

2 cloves garlic, very thinly sliced

½ teaspoon salt

Freshly ground black pepper to
taste

SERVES 6 The Italians call Jerusalem artichokes *topinambur*, the French word for the vegetable and a corruption of the name of the tribe of Brazilian Indians, Tupinambàs, who first discovered them. (The name *Jerusalem artichoke* is a corruption of *girasole*, the Italian word for sunflower—the source of these delicate, artichoke-flavored tubers.) Jerusalem artichokes—sometimes called sunchokes in this country, just to confuse the issue—by any name, are wonderful prepared in this traditionally Piemontese way. I once ate a salad like this at the Osteria del Buongustaio in a town called Bra in the Piemonte Roero hills. It was served over paper-thin slices of poached chicken. *Divino.*

1. Put the cream in a small, heavy-bottomed nonreactive saucepan and simmer to reduce by half, about 15 minutes. Remove from heat and let cool.

2. Add the juice of 1 lemon to a large bowl filled with cold water. Peel the artichokes and add them to the lemon water as you finish each one.

3. Combine the juice of the remaining lemon and a few ice cubes in another large bowl filled with cold water. Use a mandoline or a vegetable peeler to very thinly slice the tubers. Add to the lemon water as you finish each one. When all of the chokes have been sliced, transfer them, using a slotted spoon, to several layers of paper towels to drain. Pat dry.

4. In a small skillet over low heat, combine the olive oil, anchovies, and garlic. Cook, stirring with a wooden spoon, until the anchovies dissolve. Remove from heat and let cool.

5. In a large bowl, combine the artichokes, reduced cream, anchovy mixture, the 1 tablespoon lemon juice, the salt, and a few grinds of pepper. Toss together. Taste and adjust the seasoning. Serve at room temperature.

INSALATA DI RISO ALLA NOVARESE

[Rice Salad in the Style of Novara]

1½ cups Carnaroli or a long-grain rice, cooked, drained, and cooled

1 tablespoon olive oil

3 anchovy fillets

1 clove garlic, very thinly sliced

2 tablespoons white-truffle scented olive oil

4 teaspoons fresh lemon juice

2 tablespoons minced fresh flat-leaf parsley

1 ounce preserved black truffles, thinly sliced

¼ teaspoon salt

Radicchio leaves for serving

SERVES 6 Food in Italy is fiercely regional, and each province, city, town, and village thinks that what it produces is the most *eccezionale.* The contest over who produces the best rice is no exception to this competition: Pavia or Mantova in Lombardia? Or Vercelli or Novara in Piemonte? To my palate, however, they're all equally good. ⅏ This salad, a specialty of Novara, is one of the priciest in the book because of the truffles that are the featured ingredient. But a book dedicated to Italian salads just has to include this one.

1. Put the cooked rice in a large bowl and set aside.

2. In a small skillet over low heat, combine the olive oil, anchovies, and garlic. Cook, without frying, stirring with a wooden spoon, just until the anchovies dissolve. Remove from heat and let cool for a few minutes.

3. Add the anchovy mixture, truffle oil, lemon juice, parsley, sliced truffles, and salt to the rice. Toss to thoroughly combine. Serve at room temperature on a bed of radicchio.

NOTE: Order preserved black truffles and white truffle-scented olive oil from Dean and DeLuca (www.dean-deluca.com, or 1-800-221-7714).

INSALATA DI FONTINA E PEPERONI GIALLI

[Fontina and Roasted Yellow Pepper Salad]

6 yellow bell peppers

2 tablespoons olive oil

2 tablespoons heavy cream

1 teaspoon Dijon mustard

½ teaspoon salt

Freshly ground black pepper to taste

⅔ pound imported Fontina cheese (from Val d'Aosta), cut into 1½-inch matchsticks

½ cup coarsely chopped green olives

SERVES 6 Here's another interesting antipasto salad from the Piemonte region of northwestern Italy. It was specifically created to showcase fragrant, nutty-flavored Italian Fontina cheese, which comes from Val d'Aosta. This salad is sometimes simply called *insalata di formaggio.* ⳾ When roasted, the sweet yellow peppers take on a subtle smokiness that's a perfect contrast to the cheese.

1. Roast the whole peppers over a gas flame, turning until completely charred. Put in a bowl, cover the bowl with plastic wrap, and let cool for at least 30 minutes.

2. In a small bowl, combine the olive oil, heavy cream, mustard, salt, and a couple of grinds of pepper. Whisk together until emulsified. Set aside.

3. Peel the skin from the peppers and discard the cores, seeds, and membranes. Cut the peppers into ¼-inch-wide strips.

4. In a large bowl, combine the peppers, cheese, olives, and cream mixture. Toss together. Serve at room temperature.

INSALATA DI PATATE CON CAPPERI E ACCIUGHE

[Potato Salad with Capers and Anchovies]

2½ pounds small white potatoes
½ cup extra-virgin olive oil
2 teaspoons red wine vinegar
¼ cup coarsely chopped fresh
    flat-leaf parsley
2 tablespoons capers
2 anchovy fillets, minced
Salt and freshly ground black
    pepper to taste

SERVES 6 My constant quizzing of Italian friends about their favorite salads was almost always answered with this one, among others. It's a special favorite of my friend from Salerno, Antonia Jannone, and her daughter, Viola Vergani. Viola studies acting in New York and has worked in my catering kitchen from time to time. This is the salad Viola invariably makes when we need a quick lunch.

1. Cook the potatoes in a large pot of boiling water for about 20 minutes, or until a tester easily passes through them. Drain, reserving some of the cooking water. Carefully peel the potatoes while they're still hot. Cut them into ¼-inch-thick slices and put them in a large bowl.

2. Add the olive oil and vinegar to the still-warm potatoes. Toss to thoroughly combine. If the mixture seems a bit dry, add a few tablespoons of the hot potato water. Let sit for 10 minutes.

3. Add the parsley, capers, and anchovies to the bowl. Toss to combine. Taste for salt and add with pepper as needed.

INSALATA CALABRESE

[Baked-Potato Salad from Calabria]

2 pounds baking potatoes (about
   3 large potatoes)
1 green bell pepper, seeded, de-
   ribbed, and cut into fine julienne
1 large Bermuda, Vidalia, or other
   sweet white onion, cut into
   ¼-inch-wide slices
¼ cup extra-virgin olive oil
1 teaspoon salt

SERVES 4 TO 6 This simple potato salad is a classic Calabrese dish traditionally made with the highly flavored onions from Tropea, on the region's west coast. I've made it with Bermuda onions, as well as with Vidalias. The results were equally good. This salad is unique in using baking potatoes. In Calabria, the potatoes are often baked in the ashes of an outdoor oven, lending a smoky flavor to the salad.

1. Preheat an oven to 400°F. Prick the potatoes with a fork and place them on the middle rack of the oven. Bake for 30 to 40 minutes, or until almost cooked through but still firm; a tester should pass through with a tiny bit of resistance. As they cool, they'll cook a little more.

2. Peel the potatoes while still warm and cut them into ¼-inch-thick rounds. Put them in a large bowl. Add the pepper, onion, oil, and salt. Using a rubber spatula, carefully toss together to combine. Serve immediately, or keep at room temperature for up to 2 hours before serving.

INSALATA DI PATATE ALLA PELLEGRINO ARTUSI

[Pellegrino Artusi's Potato Salad]

1½ pounds medium white
   potatoes

2 tablespoons minced celery
   (Artusi says *minutissime*, which is
   tiny, tiny)

1 tablespoon minced pickled onion

2 tablespoons minced cornichons

2 tablespoons finely diced red
   pepper

2 anchovy fillets, minced

1 tablespoon minced capers

1 tablespoon minced fresh basil

1 teaspoon dried oregano

2 hard-cooked eggs

½ cup extra-virgin olive oil

1 teaspoon red wine vinegar

1 teaspoon salt

½ teaspoon freshly ground black
   pepper

SERVES 6 In 1891, Pellegrino Artusi wrote *La Scienza in Cucina, e l'Arte di Mangiare Bene*, the seminal modern-day Italian cookbook. *Culinary Science, and the Art of Eating Well* contains more than 750 recipes that reflect the vast range of Italian cuisine. From the northernmost province there is a *minestra di krapfen* (a soup with dumplings), and from Sicily a *pasticcio a sorpresa* (baked pasta filled with "surprise" ingredients). Included in each recipe is an editorial comment or a history lesson from author Artusi. His *insalata di patate* contains an irresistible comment: "Even although we're only talking about potatoes, this modest dish is destined to be praised—but it's not for all stomachs." (Too many pickled ingredients?) I find it indeed highly commendable, *and* also quite digestible.

1. Cook the potatoes in abundant boiling water until a tester easily passes through them. Drain on paper towels.

2. In a large bowl, combine the celery, onion, cornichons, red pepper, anchovies, capers, basil, and oregano.

3. Using a chef's knife, finely chop the hard-cooked eggs, then use the side of the knife to smash the chopped egg into a coarse paste. Add the egg paste to the vegetable mixture. Add the olive oil, vinegar, salt, and pepper and stir with a fork to thoroughly combine.

4. Peel the potatoes, cut them into 1-inch chunks, and add them to the bowl. Toss until the potatoes are coated with the other ingredients. Serve immediately. Or, in Artusi's final words, ". . . *è un piatto che può conservarsi per diversi giorni.*" ("It's a dish that lasts for a few days"). Store in a tightly covered container in the refrigerator for up to 3 days.

MACEDONIA DEI FRUTTI DEL FRUTTETO CON SALSA DI CACHI

[Macedoine of Orchard Fruits with Persimmon Sauce]

PERSIMMON SAUCE:

2 very ripe Hachiya or Fuyu
  persimmons, halved

1 tablespoon fresh lemon juice

½ cup sugar

2 tablespoons fresh lemon juice

4 Bosc, Anjou, Bartlett, or other fall
  pears

4 Fuji, Delicious, Winesap, or other
  fall apples

1 cup pomegranate seeds

SERVES 8 *Macedoine* is a French culinary term for a salad of mixed diced fruits or vegetables. The word is fittingly derived from the now-independent state of Macedonia, where people of varied ethnicities and religions have historically lived together in relative harmony. ⫸ Italian fruit macedoines, a dessert staple in most restaurants, trattorias, and homes, are particularly good with fall fruit. When I visit Italy in the fall or early winter, I'm dazzled and delighted with the abundance of pomegranates and persimmons that literally fall off the trees and cover the streets of many towns. This macedoine incorporates the fruits of an Italian autumn.

1. To make the sauce: Discard the seeds from the persimmons and carefully scrape the pulp from the skins. Put the pulp in a small bowl. Add the 1 tablespoon lemon juice and the sugar. Stir to combine. Set aside.

2. Put the 2 tablespoons lemon juice in a large bowl. Peel, core, and dice the pears and apples one at a time, adding each to the bowl and tossing with the lemon juice to keep the fruit from turning brown.

3. Add the pomegranate seeds and persimmon sauce to the bowl of fruit and toss to thoroughly combine. Serve immediately, or refrigerate in a tightly covered container for up to 3 days. Bring to room temperature before serving.

4

Wintertime in Italy means that the greens turn red—

literally. The quintessential wintertime salad ingredient, radicchio,

which appears as *rosso di Treviso*, *rosso di Chioggia*, and *variegato di*

Castelfranco, is harvested not fully mature and still green. It's then that

the process called *imbianchiamento* (blanching) begins. The bunches

of green radicchio are taken to darkened warehouses, where they

are grown in sterilized sand until they mature and form their

characteristic shapes. Next, they are put in large tubs with running

water until they turn red, and are ready for the market and the kitchen,

where they star in some of the most ingenious of all Italian salads.

[Cabbage and Apples from Alto Adige]

1 pound green cabbage, quartered, cored, and finely shredded

2 tart green apples such as Granny Smith, quartered, cored, and thinly sliced

1 onion, thinly sliced

1 clove garlic, mashed through a press

2 tablespoons fresh lemon juice

¼ pound smoked slab bacon, cut into ¼-inch dice

2 tablespoons olive oil

2 teaspoons cider vinegar

½ teaspoon fennel seeds

1 teaspoon salt

½ teaspoon freshly ground black pepper

SERVES 6 TO 8 Alto Adige is in the part of Italy known as the *sud-tirol*—the southern Tyrol—which was part of the Austro-Hungarian Empire until after World War I, when it was annexed to Italy, much to the chagrin of the Austrians. Now, traditions mix amicably. Apple strudel is as much a part of *la cucina sud-tirolese* as polenta. Along with wine grapes, apples are the main agricultural harvest of the Alto Adige. In spring, the orchards are a magnificent vision when the trees are in bloom with the flowers that are the source for this region's world-famous, apple-blossom honey; fall brings a great apple harvest, and the cider vinegar that is part of so many salad dressings in the north.

1. In a large bowl, combine the cabbage, apples, onion, garlic, and lemon juice. Toss and set aside.

2. In a small skillet over medium heat, cook the bacon until brown and crispy. Using a slotted spoon, transfer to paper towels to drain. Pour off all but 1 tablespoon of the bacon fat. Add the olive oil to the skillet and then immediately pour the fat mixture over the cabbage. Add the bacon bits, vinegar, fennel seeds, salt, and pepper. Using a rubber spatula, carefully toss the ingredients together. Let sit at room temperature for at least 30 minutes or up to 1 hour before serving.

INSALATA DI NATALE ALLA MARINA

[Marina's Christmas Salad]

2 tablespoons fresh lemon juice

2 ripe avocados, peeled, pitted, and cut into 1-inch chunks

2 tablespoons olive oil

¼ pound Emmentaler cheese, cut into 1-inch-long matchsticks

½ cup pomegranate seeds

½ teaspoon salt

3 cups tightly packed torn arugula leaves

SERVES 4 TO 6 Of all the recipes I tested one cold winter Sunday and distributed to neighbors to taste, this one was the clear winner. ⅏ I'm not surprised that this salad, which looks like a deconstructed wreath and tastes like a holiday, came out on top—after all, Marina Danieli, born Prada, is its inventor. Marina likes nothing better than to share good food and conversation with her husband, Bruno, family, and friends. I'm happy that she shared her family's favorite festive salad with me. ⅏ Search hard for the unusual ingredient in this one: a pomegranate. The color and texture that it adds to the salad is incomparable.

1. In a large bowl, combine the lemon juice and avocado. Toss to coat the avocado.

2. Add the olive oil, cheese, pomegranate seeds, salt, and arugula. Toss to thoroughly combine. Serve immediately.

INSALATA D'UGO

[Ugo's Salad]

6 cups tightly packed torn
radicchio leaves
1 cup cooked borlotti, kidney, or
cannellini beans
1 tablespoon olive oil
¼ pound pancetta or slab bacon,
cut into ¼-inch dice
1 tablespoon balsamic vinegar
Salt and freshly ground black
pepper to taste

SERVES 6 Ivana Zanon, proprietor of the prettiest little hotel in the Veneto, told me that this was the favorite salad of her late husband, Ugo. The Hotel Abbazia, home to the Zanon family and their lucky guests, is in the tiny town of Follina, a twenty-minute drive from Treviso. The famous *rosso di Treviso*, a kind of radicchio, is found in almost every salad in the region and is also depicted on ceramic plates, platters, bowls, pitchers, fabrics, and paper. There's no doubt that it's the preferred salad for all the Veneti—Ugo just happened to get it right when he combined it with beans and bacon.

1. In a large bowl, combine the radicchio and beans.

2. In a medium skillet over medium heat, combine the olive oil and bacon and cook until the pieces are dark brown and crisp. Turn off the heat and add the vinegar. There will be pungent vapors from the vinegar's contact with the hot fat. Immediately add the mixture to the other ingredients. Toss to combine. Taste for salt and add with freshly ground black pepper as needed. Serve immediately.

INSALATA DI RINFORZO

[Enriched Salad]

1½ pounds cauliflower, cut into
   florets (about 6 cups)

4 tablespoons capers

3 tablespoons coarsely chopped
   black olives

1 tablespoon chopped anchovies

4 tablespoons coarsely chopped
   pickled vegetables (*sottaceti*, or
   giardiniera)

¼ cup extra-virgin olive oil

2 teaspoons red wine vinegar

½ teaspoon salt

½ teaspoon freshly ground black
   pepper

OPTIONAL ADDITIONS:

Coarsely chopped escarole

Hardtack biscuits (*gallette da
   marinaio*, or *taralli*, available in
   Italian bakeries)

Green olives

Steamed carrot rounds

SERVES 6 This salad, which is sometimes called *caponata*, has nothing to do with the Sicilian caponata (page 74) made with eggplant that's so familiar to us in the United States. *Insalata di rinforzo*, a traditional Christmastime salad that uses early-winter cauliflower as its main ingredient, is from Campania, the region that has Naples as its capital. It's called *rinforzo* (enriched) because every day new ingredients can be added to the leftover salad.

1. In a large saucepan fitted with a metal steamer, steam the cauliflower florets over medium heat until a tester easily passes through them. Remove from the steamer and let cool.

2. Put the cauliflower into a large bowl. Add the capers, black olives, anchovies, pickled vegetables, olive oil, vinegar, salt, and pepper. Toss together to thoroughly combine.

3. Add any of the optional ingredients you like. For example, you could place the salad on a bed of chopped escarole and surround it with the hardtack and green olives.

3 tablespoons olive oil

2 teaspoons white truffle olive oil

1 teaspoon red wine vinegar

2 teaspoons fresh lemon juice

2 teaspoons Dijon mustard

½ teaspoon salt

6 cups tightly packed torn
   radicchio leaves

½ ounce preserved black truffles,
   thinly sliced

SERVES 6 The brilliant composer of the classic *Il Barbiere di Siviglia*, Gioacchino Rossini, was born in 1792 in the Marches. This salad recipe, which he sent to a friend, also became a classic. One taste and you'll understand why *il maestro* Rossini was given the honorary title *Il Re dei Funghi*, The King of Mushrooms. ⽘ Rossini wrote: ". . . Take oil from Provence, some English mustard, vinegar from France, a little lemon juice, salt and pepper: whisk and mix together, then add a few truffles cut into very thin slices. The truffles form a kind of halo of flavor that will send the gourmand into ecstasy." ⽘ In Italy, this salad is made with fresh white truffles, which are rare and extremely expensive in the United States. The combination of preserved black truffles and white truffle oil creates a good effect.

1. In a large bowl, combine the olive oil, truffle oil, vinegar, lemon juice, mustard, and salt. Whisk together until emulsified. Add the radicchio and truffles. Toss together to thoroughly combine. Serve immediately.

NOTE: Preserved black truffles and white truffle-scented olive oil are available from Dean and DeLuca (www.dean-deluca.com; 1-800-221-7714).

INSALATA DI FINOCCHIO E OLIVE VERDI

[Fennel and Green Olive Salad]

3 tablespoons extra-virgin olive oil

2 teaspoons red wine vinegar

1 clove garlic, smashed

1 teaspoon salt

2 fennel bulbs, trimmed, halved lengthwise, and thinly sliced

1 cup coarsely chopped celery leaves

1 cup (¼ pound) green Sicilian olives, pitted and coarsely chopped

2 tablespoons coarsely chopped fresh mint

SERVES 6 Fresh raw fennel is often added to the fruit bowl and served as dessert in Italy. The aromatic, licorice-flavored vegetable is a great digestive. This Sicilian fennel salad, which also includes celery leaves and fresh mint, other digestion aids, would be a perfect conclusion to a rich meal.

1. In a small bowl, combine the olive oil, vinegar, garlic, and salt. Whisk together until emulsified. Let stand at room temperature for at least 1 hour or up to 8 hours to let the garlic flavor fully develop before adding it to the vegetables.

2. In a large bowl, combine the fennel, celery leaves, olives, and mint. Remove the garlic clove from the vinaigrette. Add the vinaigrette to the fennel mixture. Toss together to thoroughly combine. Serve immediately.

INSALATA DI ARANCE ALLA TREVIGIANA

[Orange Salad, Treviso Style]

4 oranges, peeled and segmented
   (see page 31)
2 leeks (white part only), halved
   lengthwise
3 cups tightly packed torn
   radicchio leaves
2 tablespoons olive oil
2 teaspoons cider vinegar
1 teaspoon Dijon mustard
1 teaspoon honey
½ teaspoon salt
½ teaspoon freshly ground white
   pepper

SERVES 4 TO 6 When oranges from Sicily and radicchio from the Veneto appear on the greengrocers' shelves in Italy, winter is on its way. The oranges arrive individually wrapped in decorated (and collectible) papers that announce their variety, either Tarocco or Moro. Radicchio is identified by the names of the area where it's grown. The beautiful pale-green leaf with rose-colored brushstrokes is *variegato di Castelfranco*; the long, skinny carmine leaf is *rosso di Treviso*, while the tight round red head that we're used to seeing in the United States is *rosso di Chioggia*. This salad comes from Treviso.

1. Put the orange segments in a large bowl.

2. Rinse the leeks in a bowl of water, lifting them up and down a few times to make sure all the grit is removed. Rinse them under running water and drain on paper towels. Cut the leeks into fine julienne. Add the leeks and radicchio to the bowl with the oranges.

3. In a small bowl, combine the olive oil, vinegar, mustard, honey, salt, and pepper. Whisk together until emulsified. Add to the other ingredients and toss to thoroughly combine. Serve immediately.

INSALATA DI ARANCE, OLIVE NERE, E ARINGHE

[Salad with Oranges, Black Olives, and Herring]

½ red onion, thinly sliced

¼ cup extra-virgin olive oil

2 teaspoons red wine vinegar

1 teaspoon dried oregano

½ teaspoon salt

¼ teaspoon ground red hot pepper

3 cups tightly packed torn escarole leaves

4 blood oranges or navel oranges, peeled and cut into ¼-inch-thick slices, then halved crosswise

¾ pound Mediterranean salted herring, smoked bluefish, or smoked trout, cut into ¾-inch pieces (about 1¼ cups)

¼ cup coarsely chopped pitted black olives, such as kalamata

SERVES 6 This is an adaptation of a recipe by cooking teacher Anna Tasca Lanza. She told me, "... this may be the first salad invented by the Arabs when they brought the first oranges to Sicily. It's the marriage of flavors—the sweet-tart of the oranges and the saltiness of the herring—that makes this absolutely special. The escarole is my personal addition. Its slightly bitter taste makes the dish even more exquisite...." ⑅ The salted herring is a bit problematic for us in the United States. The most widely available salted herring comes from the North Atlantic, and it's very strongly flavored. Unless you can find milder-tasting Mediterranean salted herring or sardines, use smoked bluefish or smoked trout instead.

1. Soak the onion in a small bowl of salted ice water for at least 30 minutes or up to 1 hour to remove some of the bite.

2. In a large bowl, combine the olive oil, vinegar, oregano, salt, and pepper. Whisk together until emulsified.

3. Add the escarole, oranges, fish, and olives to the bowl. Drain the onions and squeeze them dry. Add them to the bowl. Toss to thoroughly combine. Serve immediately.

INSALATA PALERMITANA

[Orange and Fennel Salad from Palermo]

½ red onion, thinly sliced

3 tablespoons extra-virgin olive oil

2 teaspoons fruity vinegar such as blackberry or raspberry

1 teaspoon salt

¼ teaspoon freshly ground black pepper or ground red hot pepper

1 bulb fennel, trimmed (reserve fronds), halved lengthwise, and cut into thin crosswise slices

4 blood oranges or navel oranges, peeled and cut into ¼-inch-thick slices, then halved crosswise

¼ cup coarsely chopped pitted black olives, such as kalamata

SERVES 6 This is a first-generation descendant of Insalata di Arance, Olive Nere, e Aringhe (previous page), fennel being a relatively recent arrival to Sicily (several hundred years ago is recent in Sicily!). Though it's a typically Sicilian salad, I ate it for the first time in the home of Miro Silvera, one of my Milanese friends. This recipe reflects Miro's preference for fruity vinegar.

1. Soak the onion in a small bowl of salted ice water for at least 30 minutes or up to 1 hour to remove some of the bite.

2. In a large bowl, combine the olive oil, vinegar, salt, and pepper. Whisk together until emulsified.

3. Coarsely chop the reserved fennel fronds. Add the oranges, fennel, fennel fronds, and olives to the dressing. Drain the onions and squeeze them dry. Add the onions to the bowl. Toss to thoroughly combine. Serve immediately.

LUMIE DI SICILIA

[The Lights of Sicily]

4 navel oranges or 6 blood oranges
  (or a combination)

2 large lemons

1 large pink grapefruit

2 tablespoons finely chopped pitted kalamata olives

3 tablespoons extra-virgin olive oil

1 teaspoon salt

Fresh mint leaves for garnish
  (optional)

SERVES 6 I can't think of a more appropriate name for this lumi-nescent salad. The colorful, fragrant, and bright-tasting combination of citrus that goes into this dish is Sicily's main agricultural harvest. There's ample evidence that the first oranges—a bitter variety called a *bigarade*—were brought to Italy, via India, by Roman traders in A.D. 100. Oranges as we know them arrived with the Saracen invasion of Sicily. Lemons arrived about five hundred years later, while the grape-fruit, a relatively modern hybrid, wasn't introduced to Italian soil until the nineteenth century. ⑈ This citrus salad is based on a recipe I found in a Sicilian cookbook. It's delicious with grilled fish.

1. Cut the top and bottom from each citrus fruit down to the flesh. Setting a fruit on end, use a very sharp knife to cut off just the zest. Next, cut off the white pith down to flesh. Repeat with all the remaining fruits. You may need to use your fingers to peel any remaining pith.

2. Cut the fruit into ¼-inch-thick slices. Cut the orange and lemon slices into quarters. Cut the grapefruit slices into sixths. Put the cut fruit in a large bowl.

3. Add the chopped olives, olive oil, and salt to the fruit and toss to thoroughly combine. Serve in a shallow bowl, surrounded by mint leaves, if you like.

INSALATA DI RISO ALLA CALIFORNIA

[Rice Salad California Style]

1½ cups Carnaroli or a long-grain rice, cooked, drained, and cooled

5 blood oranges, peeled and segmented (see page 31)

1 cup coarsely chopped pitted prunes

1 rounded tablespoon coarsely chopped fresh mint

2 teaspoons Dijon mustard

1 tablespoon fresh orange juice

2 tablespoons white wine vinegar

2 tablespoons extra-virgin olive oil

1 teaspoon salt

½ teaspoon freshly ground white pepper

Radicchio leaves for serving

Fresh mint leaves for garnish

SERVES 4 TO 6 While Italy boasts some of the best dried fruit I've tasted, it seems that Italians, just like the rest of us, are intrigued by what's foreign. In this salad, prunes imported from California, exotic fare for the inhabitants of the boot, are given a place of honor. ⑅ The gorgeous raspberry-colored and -flavored blood oranges also featured in this salad are now grown in California, making them more available in the United States than in the past. All the more reason to call this salad *riso alla California.*

1. Put the rice in a large bowl. Add the orange sections, prunes, and mint.

2. In a small bowl, combine the mustard, orange juice, vinegar, olive oil, salt, and pepper. Whisk together until emulsified. Add to the rice mixture and toss to thoroughly combine. Serve on a bed of radicchio. Scatter a few mint leaves over and around the rice.

TONNO E FAGIOLI

[Tuna and Beans]

1 cup thinly sliced red onion

12 ounces Italian tuna packed in oil, drained and flaked

2½ cups cooked borlotti, kidney, or cannellini beans, or a combination

3 tablespoons extra-virgin olive oil

1 tablespoon fresh lemon juice

1 tablespoon balsamic vinegar

1 teaspoon dried oregano or sage

Freshly ground black pepper to taste

Assorted greens for serving (optional)

SERVES 4 *"Mangiamo con scatole"* ("Let's eat using canned foods") is a more and more frequent way to prepare meals in Italy. Using canned tuna and beans, you have Italian fast food supreme. *Certo* (of course), in Italy the canned tuna and beans are exceptional. Look for Italian tuna packed in olive oil for this classic combo; it makes all the difference.

1. Soak the onion in a bowl of salted ice water for at least 30 minutes or up to 1 hour to remove some of the bite.

2. In a large bowl, combine the tuna, beans, olive oil, lemon juice, vinegar, oregano or sage, and pepper. Drain the onions and squeeze them dry. Add to the bowl. Toss to thoroughly combine. Serve from the bowl, or arrange on a bed of greens on a platter, if you like.

INSALATA DI POMPELMO E AVOCADO

[Grapefruit and Avocado Salad]

3 cups firmly packed torn Boston lettuce leaves

2 ripe avocados, peeled, pitted, and cut into 1-inch chunks

1 pink grapefruit, peeled and segmented (see page 31)

¼ pound Gruyère cheese, cut into 1-inch-long matchsticks

2 tablespoons coarsely chopped walnuts

2 tablespoons extra-virgin olive oil

1 tablespoon fresh lemon juice

½ teaspoon salt

¼ teaspoon red pepper flakes

SERVES 4 TO 6 I love this salad. I love the way it tastes, and I love the way it looks: all shades of pale green, and pink. It's just what the doctor ordered for a dreary winter day. I found this in a collection of Sicilian citrus fruit recipes.

1. In a large bowl, combine the lettuce, avocados, grapefruit, cheese, and walnuts.

2. In a small bowl, combine the olive oil, lemon juice, salt, and red pepper flakes. Whisk together until emulsified. Add to the lettuce mixture and toss together to thoroughly combine. Serve immediately.

INSALATA TUTTA ROSSA

[Completely Red Salad]

½ pound red beets, peeled and diced

¾ pound red cabbage, cored and finely shredded

3 tablespoons olive oil

4 anchovy fillets

1 large clove garlic, minced

1 tablespoon red wine vinegar

2 tablespoons coarsely chopped fresh flat-leaf parsley

¼ teaspoon salt

Freshly ground black pepper to taste

SERVES 6 In Italy, all the *erbivendoli* (greengrocers) and the *super-mercato* produce departments sell beets already baked in their skins. What a civilized accommodation for the cook! In fact, many Italian recipes that include beets specify *barbabietole già cotte:* already baked beets. ⅏ These days, although beets can be found year around, they star in cool-weather preparations, as with this salad. The rich scarlet color will warm you before you taste it.

1. In a medium saucepan fitted with a metal steamer, steam the beets until a tester easily passes through them. Remove the beets from the steamer and let cool.

2. Put the cabbage in a large bowl. Add the beets.

3. In a small saucepan over medium-low heat, combine the olive oil, anchovies, and garlic. Cook, stirring with a wooden spoon, until the anchovies have melted. Add to the cabbage mixture. Add the vinegar, parsley, salt, and pepper. Toss to thoroughly combine. Let stand for at least 30 minutes or up to 2 hours before serving. Or, refrigerate in a tightly covered container for up to 3 days. Bring to room temperature before serving.

INSALATA DI CAROTE ALLA KLEM

[Klem's Carrot Salad]

1¼ pounds carrots, peeled and
   shredded (about 5 cups)

2 pink grapefruits, peeled and segmented (see page 31)

1 teaspoon olive oil

½ cup hazelnuts, coarsely chopped

1 cup plain whole-milk yogurt

2 tablespoons fresh lemon juice

1 teaspoon salt

½ teaspoon freshly ground black
   pepper

SERVES 6 I call this Klem's salad because she gave me the recipe. Klem Reginiano, born in Monza, resident of Milan, answered my query for favorite salad recipes with this one, which she said she got from a *cuoca del TV*, a television cook. ⑊ A bit like our American carrot and raisin salad—because it combines carrots with fruit—this one has a decidedly Italian personality, thanks to the toasted hazelnuts and grapefruit. ⑊ This is a wonderful first-course salad when served on a bed of Boston lettuce.

1. Put the carrots in a large bowl. Cut each grapefruit section into 3 pieces and add to the carrots.

2. Add the olive oil to a small skillet over medium heat and sauté the hazelnuts until they become bronze and smell like freshly popped corn, about 90 seconds. Add to the carrot mixture.

3. In a small bowl, whisk the yogurt, lemon juice, salt, and pepper together. Add to the carrot mixture and toss together to thoroughly combine. Serve immediately. If making ahead, delete the nuts and refrigerate the salad in a tightly covered container for up to 3 days. Add the nuts just before serving.

RINGRAZIAMENTI
[Acknowledgments]

I was thrilled to have the opportunity to write this book. The subject, salads, and the country, Italy, are topics of great interest and passion for me. ⅏ Without the help and cooperation of this group of people the task would have been impossible: *Alla favolosa* Gianna, aka Marian Young, my agent—next year at Harry's Bar! Bill LeBlond at Chronicle Books, part Italian I'm sure (his appetite). Amy Treadwell and Michele Fuller, also at Chronicle; and Deb Miner. ⅏ *Amico da anni*, friend of many years, photographer Manfredi Bellati—how nice to have worked together, *finalmente.* ⅏ Old Italian friends who with that particular brand of Italian generosity that knows no bounds gave me whatever I asked of them—and more: Gabrio and Genevieve Bini, Nino and Ester Bini, Massimo Vitali, Klem Reginiano, Paolo Rinaldi, Anna Tasca Lanza, Marijke Guidobono-Cavalchini, Clemy Vizzer, Ivana Zanon, Loredana Lazzarini, Antonia Jannone, Viola Vergani, and Marina Danieli. Thanks also to new acquaintances Lucia Piccini, Carlo Ferrero, and Maria Paleari Henssler at the riseria "La Veneria"; Dott. Guido Guardigli, Samantha Guardigli, and Matteo Zambon. ⅏ Stateside, I'm grateful for Sabrina Reisinger's invaluable kitchen assistance and Sue Kirby's computer acumen. ⅏ Miro Silvera was always there to respond to my inquiries via fax and phone, and to contribute recipes. *Miro, sei un vero amico di cuore.* ⅏ Nally Bellati, old friend, generous to a fault, hosted me at her homes in Milan and in the Veneto, contributed recipes and ideas, and was my steadfast connection to Italy throughout the creation of this book. ⅏ *E senza dubbio*, thanks to my sister Laura still answering questions. ⅏ *A tutti*—to everyone—*Mille Grazie.*